G000150778

CONTENTS

ACKNOWLEDGEMENTS

This book would not have been possible without the help of a great number of people: Peter Fuller granted access to the extensive legal files relating to the case; Attorney Edward S. Bonnie was generous with his time and resources; Phyllis Rogers, associate librarian at the Keeneland Library, helped me locate information in what is almost certainly the largest collection of *Daily Racing Forms* and *Morning Telegraphs* in existence anywhere; Christopher Goodlett, curator of the research library at the Kentucky Derby Museum in Louisville, Kentucky, tracked down notes and interviews from the collection of the late Jim Bolus, who championed the cause of Dancer's Image through the years; former reporter Billy Reed shared his recollections of the 1968 Derby; Neil Chethik, writer in residence at the Carnegie Center in Lexington, Kentucky, has mentored me through a variety of writing projects; Sally Jump, clerk of the Franklin Circuit Court; Denise Shanks, reference librarian at the Lexington Public Library; the staff at the Kentucky Department for Libraries and Archives; Stacy Bearse, former publisher of the *Blood-Horse*; Anne Keogh, chief photographer at the *Blood-Horse*; Mark Simon, editor of the *Thoroughbred Times*; everyone at The History Press; and last but not least, my wife, Roberta. Her support has been immeasurable.

INTRODUCTION

A t the head of the stretch, riding one of the favorites in the most important horse race in the world, jockey Bobby Ussery dropped his whip.

It was an accident—one of those unfortunate things that just happen sometimes—but it could not have come at a worse point in the race for Ussery. The veteran jockey had hustled Dancer's Image up from dead last in the field of fourteen, weaving through horses on the final turn like the legendary "Crazy Legs" Hirsch. When a hole opened up on the rail, Ussery cut to the inside toward clear running room. That was when the stick fell from his grasp. One second Ussery had the whip clutched in his right hand, waving it at the horse's flank; the next second it was gone. Dancer's Image was in gear, moving fast on the leaders, but the strapping gray colt still had the pacesetter and the favorite to catch.

And, suddenly, his jockey had no whip.

It happened so quickly that hardly anyone in the stands noticed. Even when watching a replay of the race, Ussery's gaffe is not obvious unless you know just when to pay attention.

"I didn't even know I lost it," Ussery told reporters after the race. "They tell me I dropped it at the three-sixteenths pole."[1]

In other circumstances, it might have sounded like an idle boast from a rider trying to cover up what could have been a fatal mistake in a major race. But it was not that at all; Ussery was simply stating a fact. He did not need the stick because Dancer's Image was good enough to win on his own.

The official *Daily Racing Form* chart for the 1968 Kentucky Derby refers to Ussery's "vigorous hand ride" in the stretch after the rider lost his whip, but those words pale in comparison to what actually happened through the final quarter mile. Crouched low over the horse's neck, his sights set on the leaders, Ussery was riding hard, pushing Dancer's Image with his legs, his hands and his voice. He kept the colt tight on the rail, and Dancer's Image surged to the front in the final furlong. He drew clear and won by 1½ lengths. The chart caller for the *Form* said that Dancer's Image was "hard pressed" to beat the favorite, Calumet Farm's Forward Pass, but that assessment belies a dramatic stretch run dominated by the winner. There was little doubt that the big, gray colt was the best horse that day.

Ussery's masterful ride in the ninety-fourth Kentucky Derby marked an important milestone for the Oklahoma native, who became the first winner of back-to-back Kentucky Derbys in more than sixty years. Eddie Arcaro won the race five times, but he could not win two in a row and neither could four-time winner Bill Hartack. Ussery's victory the previous year on long shot Proud Clarion had been an unlikely one; a year later, Ussery was confident the long stretch run at Churchill Downs favored Dancer's Image and the colt's heart-stopping, come-from-behind running style. Before the race, Ussery predicted that Dancer's Image would "be there at the wire."

He could not have been more right.

The win was a dream come true for Boston automobile dealer Peter Fuller, who bred and owned Dancer's Image, and for veteran Canadian trainer Lou Cavalaris Jr., who nursed the colt's sore ankles through a demanding three-year-old campaign and got him to the Derby sound enough to win. Dancer's Image was the first Kentucky Derby starter for both men, and the broad smiles on their faces, as they led the colt into the Churchill Downs winner's circle, showed how much they were savoring the moment. Curiously, though, in some of the photographs, Cavalaris is staring down, apparently assessing the Derby winner's fragile front ankles.

The $5,000 gold trophy awarded to the winning owner each year was the holy grail of Thoroughbred racing, and it belonged to Fuller—for a while, at least. As events unfolded, keeping the coveted Derby trophy would prove far more difficult than winning it.

Later that evening, more than one hundred people showed up for the traditional winner's celebration hosted by Churchill Downs president Wathen Knebelkamp. Fuller was the life of the party—and for good reason. Only one three-year-old is good enough to win the Kentucky Derby each year, and in 1968, that horse was Dancer's Image.

"I'm truly happy about this," Fuller told reporters gathered around the table that he shared with his family. "I love winning, but others have to lose. And that's very tough. Isn't it, kids?"[2]

While the party was in full swing in the track's private dining room, there was activity of another kind going on in the barn area. A lab technician toiling in a cramped trailer was mixing chemicals with urine samples collected from the winners of each race on Derby Day. One of the numbered samples— the technician at the time did not know from which horse—unexpectedly changed color when the reagent was added. It was a preliminary screening test, not specific for any particular prohibited medication, but the color change indicated that something was wrong.

On Tuesday, three days after Knebelkamp lifted a glass to toast Peter Fuller as the owner of the Derby winner, the track president announced that Dancer's Image had tested positive for phenylbutazone, an anti-inflammatory drug prohibited under the rules of racing in Kentucky. The winner's share of the purse, Knebelkamp said, now would go to the second-place horse, Calumet Farm's Forward Pass.

The Kentucky Derby is rightfully called the "most exciting two minutes in sports," but hearings and lawsuits would drag on for five years before anyone could say for sure whether Dancer's Image or Forward Pass "officially" won the 1968 running of the race. Decades after Forward Pass finally was awarded the winner's purse and the gold trophy, there still are more questions than answers about what really happened on that first Saturday in May. The mystery may never be resolved.

Chapter 1

THE COMMONER AND
THE KING

A man with $20,000 in his pocket could buy a lot in 1964.

A gallon of regular gasoline cost $0.30 that year. A loaf of bread was $0.21 at the local market; a full-blown turkey dinner at Howard Johnson's was $1.49; and first-class postage for a letter was $0.05. The average worker took home $6,000.00 a year; a nice house cost $13,000.00; rent for a two-bedroom apartment in Los Angeles was $120.00 a month; and a five-night Hawaiian cruise on the Matson Line was $414.00. Tuition at Harvard was $2,400.00 a year. You could catch Carol Channing on Broadway for $10.00 or buy a ticket to see Sean Connery as James Bond in *Goldfinger* for $1.00.

Ford introduced a new sports car in 1964, the Mustang, with the sticker price of $2,368. The pony car was a bargain, considering that the average cost of an automobile hovered around $3,500. The luxury Cadillacs that graced the showroom at Peter Fuller's Boston dealership cost a little more than average, but $20,000 still would buy a pair of the automobiles, with some change left over.[3]

The going price for the privilege of sending a single Thoroughbred mare to Alfred G. Vanderbilt Jr.'s Sagamore Farm in the rolling hills north of Baltimore for a breeding to Native Dancer was also $20,000. It was an astronomical amount—the highest advertised stud fee in the world.[4]

As expensive gambles go, though, the pricey stud fee seemed like a pretty good bet, almost as safe as a ticket to win on Native Dancer at the track.

Native Dancer had been a spectacular racehorse, winning twenty-one of twenty-two races and earning Horse of the Year honors in 1952 and 1954,

Native Dancer, as a two-year-old at Saratoga. *Courtesy of the* Blood-Horse.

and ten years later, he already was well established as a sire of very good horses. Ironically, though, the horse was best known for the only race he lost, the 1953 Kentucky Derby.

Trainer Bill Winfrey brought the Vanderbilt homebred along slowly, and the horse did not make his first start as a two-year-old until late April 1952. Nine races later, with wins in the Saratoga Special, the Hopeful, the Futurity and four other stakes races to his credit, Native Dancer shared Horse of the Year honors with Belmont Stakes winner and champion three-year-old One Count. It was the first time a two-year-old ever had been voted Horse of the Year, and it was a harbinger of things to come.

If there was a knock against Native Dancer, it was the condition of his ankles, which had been a matter of some concern throughout the year. Winfrey always dismissed Native Dancer's ankle problems as little more than annoyances, in public at least, but by the end of 1952, his ankles were bothersome enough to require serious treatment in preparation for what the owner and trainer expected would be a grueling three-year-old campaign.

Native Dancer was shipped to California with the rest of the Vanderbilt stable late in 1952, and on December 1, the horse's ankles were "fired." Firing is a common and questionable practice that involves the repeated application of a very hot iron to the injured area. The idea is that the extreme inflammation that results from the firing, which can include serious third-degree burns, encourages blood flow to the area and hastens healing. It is just as likely, though, that a couple of months' enforced rest after firing does a sore horse more good than the procedure itself.

Back in New York in April 1953, Native Dancer made his first start in six months in the Gotham Stakes. The colt's reputation did not scare anyone away, and so many three-year-olds were entered that the race was split into two divisions. Native Dancer won his division by two lengths in his first start since being fired and laid up to recuperate. The Gotham was an auspicious start to the horse's three-year-old campaign and to his career as a television personality. The race was broadcast live on national television, and Native Dancer was an instant star, his dark gray coat making him easy to pick out among other horses on the black and white sets in living rooms across the country.

A week later, with forty thousand fans on hand at the old Jamaica Race Track on Long Island and millions watching the live broadcast on NBC, Native Dancer won the Wood Memorial by 4½ lengths. He raced as a betting entry with another Vanderbilt horse, Social Outcast, in the Wood, and the two horses were coupled again in the Kentucky Derby. The entry was the 3-5 favorite, and almost everyone viewed the actual running of the Derby as a mere formality, the first stop on Native Dancer's Triple Crown trail.

Then, the unthinkable happened.

Native Dancer lost.

Dark Star, a long shot at odds of 25-1, took the lead at the start of the race and stayed there, holding off a furious late charge through the stretch by Native Dancer. The placing judges flashed the PHOTO sign on the tote board, but the finish was not close enough to really warrant a second look. Native Dancer was closing strongly after a rough trip and a questionable ride from jockey Eddie Guerin, but Dark Star was a clear head in front when the horses crossed the finish line.

Native Dancer raced seven more times in 1953, winning the Preakness Stakes, the Belmont Stakes and every other major race for three-year-olds on the way to being named champion of his division. At four, he won the Metropolitan Mile under 130 pounds, the most weight the horse ever carried, and two other races before being retired. Native Dancer had been sore after the Metropolitan, and he came up lame again later in the year. Native Dancer had shared Horse of the Year honors as a two-year-old; at four, he was the unanimous choice despite his abbreviated campaign. He even appeared on the cover of *Time* magazine in 1954. The horse was inducted into the National Museum of Racing Hall of Fame in 1963.

By 1964, Native Dancer already had established himself as an outstanding young sire. His first European standout was the appropriately named filly Hula Dancer, a major winner in France as a two-year-old in 1962 and winner of the One Thousand Guineas in England in 1963. That same year, Raise a Native became Native Dancer's first North American star when the brilliantly fast colt soundly trounced every horse he faced during a spectacular but brief juvenile campaign. At the end of the year, Raise a Native shared championship honors in his division with Hurry to Market.

Raise a Native was retired due to a bowed tendon before he could race at three in 1964, a crushing disappointment for those who hoped the colt could avenge his sire's loss in the Kentucky Derby, but Native Dancer still was well represented in the classics that year. Northern Dancer, whose dam Natalma was a daughter of Native Dancer, won the Kentucky Derby in track-record time, won the Preakness Stakes and finished third in the Belmont Stakes. The stock of Native Dancer was on the rise, both literally and figuratively.

Breeders who could afford the lofty stud fee were lining up to send broodmares to Native Dancer, and Vanderbilt found himself in an unusual and enviable position. He wanted to keep Native Dancer's book of mares relatively small each

Native Dancer at stud in Maryland. *Winants Brothers photo. Courtesy of the* Blood-Horse.

year, and with the demand for matings with the popular stallion far outstripping the supply, Vanderbilt had the luxury of being able to pick and choose.

Vanderbilt certainly did not need the money generated by Native Dancer's stud fees. His late father, one of the richest men in America, was among the passengers lost when the ocean liner *Lusitania* was torpedoed by a German submarine in 1915. He left his son several million dollars at a time when one million dollars was serious money. A few years later, on Vanderbilt's twenty-first birthday, his mother made him a gift of Sagamore Farm in Maryland's lush Worthington Valley. Sorting through applications for breedings to Native Dancer every year, Vanderbilt's only concern was insuring his horse's success as a sire. He did that by packing Native Dancer's book with some of the best broodmares on two continents.

***

One of the owners petitioning Alfred Vanderbilt for a 1964 season to Native Dancer was Peter Fuller, a Boston automobile dealer who had been racing a modest stable of Thoroughbreds since the early 1950s. Fuller attended his first Kentucky Derby earlier in 1964, and he had Native Dancer on his mind. Northern Dancer won the Derby in record time, and Northern Dancer's dam, Natalma, was a daughter of the Vanderbilt stallion.

Fuller had grown accustomed to success in almost everything he did, from amateur boxing to selling Cadillacs to horse racing, but he did not take his success for granted. He worked hard for it, and he gambled when it was necessary. The $20,000 asking price for a Native Dancer season was far and away the highest stud fee Fuller had ever paid, but he wanted to upgrade the quality of his stable, and Native Dancer was an obvious ticket to the stratosphere—and perhaps to the Kentucky Derby.

A less obvious choice was the broodmare Fuller wanted to send to Sagamore Farm. Noors Image was a nice horse but, at first blush, seemed an unlikely prospect for the sizeable investment required to secure a breeding to a sire like Native Dancer. The mare was Mrs. Wallis Simpson to Native Dancer's King Edward VIII.

Noors Image had a promising two-year-old season, but she never really raced up to the level her pedigree suggested. She won twice as a juvenile in 1955 and ran second in a pair of important stakes races for two-year-old fillies in New York in the fall, the Astarita and the Frizette. Noors Image possessed a good mix of speed and stamina—the Astarita was a sprint at 6 furlongs, the Frizette was run at 1¹⁄₁₆ miles, and she held her own against good company in both of them.

In 1935, the Jockey Club started publishing a ranking of the season's best two-year-olds, assigning weights as if all the horses were running in a hypothetical race. Noors Image was one of several juvenile fillies weighted at 110 pounds on the 1955 Experimental Free Handicap, 6 pounds less than the top-weighted filly, Doubledogdare. Noors Image was not the best two-year-old filly out that year, but she was in the top tier.

The filly seemed to have a promising future on the track, but it never materialized.

She managed just two seconds and a third as a three-year-old without ever getting on the board in a stakes race. She was retired at the end of the year but returned to the track as a five-year-old when she failed to get in foal. By the time Noors Image attracted Peter Fuller's attention, she was running in low-level claiming races at Suffolk Downs. Fuller claimed the mare for $5,000 from John A. Bell III, a prominent Kentucky owner and breeder, in August 1958.

Claimers carry prices on their heads when they race and every horse is for sale when the starting gate opens. Claiming races keep owners and trainers honest because no sensible owner is going to risk losing a good horse in a cheap claiming race just to win a purse. A $5,000 claimer usually is worth just that much, nothing more.

Fuller retired Noors Image when she was five in 1958. The mare had won two races, placed in two stakes and earned $34,115, almost none of it for Fuller. The next year he bred her to Sailed Away, a lightly regarded son of Triple Crown winner and Horse of the Year War Admiral and a grandson of Man o' War. The foal from that breeding, Sailing Chance, was the best horse ever sired by Sailed Away. Sailing Chance raced mainly in New England, where he finished third in the New England Futurity in 1962 and won the New England Sophomore Stakes in 1963.

When it came time to select a mare to send to Native Dancer, Fuller settled on Noors Image, a promising but largely unproven broodmare. She had a good pedigree, a decent racing record as a two-year-old, and she had produced a stakes winner when bred to an obscure stallion that had sired only one stakes winner. It was reasonable to predict that Noors Image would do even better when bred to an outstanding stallion like Native Dancer. The question was how much better.

Noors Image also looked like she might be a good match for Vanderbilt's stallion when you compared the bloodlines of the two horses.

Noors Image, dam of Dancer's Image. *Winants Brothers photo. Courtesy of the* Blood-Horse.

Native Dancer's pedigree, going back three generations, was filled almost exclusively with horses bred in North America, while there was a distinctly European flavor to the lineage of Noors Image. Her sire, Noor, was an Irish-bred son of Nasrullah that managed to defeat Triple Crown winner Citation on three different occasions; her dam, Little Sphinx, was an American-bred daughter of the English stallion Challenger II. When a stallion and a mare share few common ancestors in the first three or four generations, it is called an "outcross" and many breeders think such a mating can produce the fastest racehorses. A Native Dancer/Noors Image mating would be a perfect outcross. A similar outcross had produced a stakes winner when Noors Image was bred to Sailed Away, so Fuller wrote the check.

Like every Thoroughbred owner, Fuller wanted to win the Kentucky Derby. Like every son, he wanted to honor his father.

***

Alvan Tufts Fuller was an overachiever decades before the term ever became fashionable. He was the epitome of a self-made man.[5]

Fuller dropped out of school when his father died and, at age sixteen, went to work in a rubber factory to earn money for the family. He might have stayed there except for uncommon ambition and a drive to succeed. Fuller parlayed a spare-time hobby into a successful bicycle shop in his hometown, and he was one of the first people on this side of the Atlantic to recognize the enormous commercial potential of a newfangled contraption called an automobile. In 1899, the same year William McKinley climbed into a Stanley Steamer and became the first United States president to ride in a car, Fuller sold the trophies he had won racing bicycles to finance a buying trip to Europe. He picked up two of the new machines, a pair of De Dion Voiturettes.

Those two vehicles were the first automobiles brought into the United States through the Port of Boston. They became the foundation for an enormously successful automobile dealership on Commonwealth Avenue in Boston, one that was voted the best in the world by 1920. Always an innovator, Fuller generally is given credit for coming up with the revolutionary ideas of buying on time and trading in an old automobile for credit on a new one. Selling cars never has been the same.

A strong commitment to public service led Fuller into politics. He served in the state legislature and in the United States House of Representatives, then as lieutenant governor of Massachusetts before ascending to the governor's mansion in 1925. Fuller reportedly never accepted a salary during his time in office, instead leaving the uncashed paychecks to his children as souvenirs.

Coming across the governor's desk in 1927 was a petition that helped define his career as a politician, a controversial clemency plea on behalf of convicted anarchists Nicola Sacco and Bartolomeo Vanzetti. The pair was facing execution for their involvement in the shooting deaths of two payroll guards during a South Braintree, Massachusetts robbery in 1920, and Governor Fuller was being asked to commute the death sentences. Questions about the trial had been on the rise, and critics argued that Sacco and Vanzetti had been convicted because of their extreme political beliefs rather than their guilt. Governor Fuller appointed Harvard president Abbott Lowell, Massachusetts Institute of Technology president Dr. Samuel Stratton and retired judge Robert Grant to review the case and advise him about the fairness of the trial.

The Lowell Committee determined that the trial and appeals had been fundamentally fair and advised against clemency. In the face of a growing wave of protests in the United States and abroad, Governor Fuller refused to commute the sentences. Sacco and Vanzetti were executed on August 23, 1927. The prospect of serious political fallout from the clemency decision, which materialized and may have sabotaged a bid for national office, did not deter Governor Fuller from making the decision he thought was the correct one.

Whether Sacco and Vanzetti actually were guilty of the killings has been a topic of heated discussion ever since their executions. Supporters of the verdicts and Governor Fuller's decision to let the death sentences stand argue that the justice system worked the way it was supposed to; critics point to discrepancies in the trial testimony and exculpatory evidence that supposedly was withheld from the defense.

That debate never will be settled. Forensic evidence from the case has deteriorated over time, and a definitive answer about what actually happened is impossible. All that remains is speculation. Controversy aside, the enduring legacy for Governor Fuller was that he held his ground and did what he thought was right, even in the face of severe criticism. Standing up for principle was a trait Fuller had in abundance, and it was a major contributor to his success. It also was one of the gifts he passed along to his children.

Fuller retired from politics after a second term as governor to devote his time to the Cadillac dealership in Boston, to expanding his art collection and to a wide range of philanthropic pursuits. He was a role model for his children, especially Peter, who, after his father's death in 1958, vowed to name a horse in honor of the man and the special relationship they shared. It would have to be a special horse, though—one good enough to represent the enormous pride and affection Peter Fuller felt for his late father.

On April 10, 1965, Noors Image produced a handsome foal from the breeding to Native Dancer. The pricey stud fee had been worth it. Fuller quickly decided this was the horse he had been waiting for and he named the colt A.T.'s Image in memory of his father, Alvan Tufts Fuller. And maybe—just maybe—Fuller now had a horse good enough to win the Kentucky Derby.

A.T.'s Image looked like a racehorse, but whether the colt had inherited his sire's blazing speed and huge heart was anybody's guess. Those questions could not be answered for a couple of years. The Kentucky Derby still was three years away. There was no doubt, though, that the colt had inherited his sire's good looks and his striking gray coat.

As it soon became apparent, though, the horse also inherited Native Dancer's questionable ankles.

Chapter 2

THOROUGHBREDS
AND BLONDES

Horse racing in the 1960s was the quintessential "old boys' club," so much so that veteran *Daily Racing Form* columnist Barney Nagler could suggest that "all good trainers of horses know that thoroughbreds, like blondes, go first in the ankles" without raising many eyebrows.[6]

Lou Cavalaris Jr. was one of those good trainers. He ran a busy public stable, conditioning horses for a dozen owners, usually at more than one track at the same time, and he was at the top of his game in 1966. He saddled more winners than any other trainer that year, and no one makes 175 trips to the winner's circle without knowing a thing or two about appreciating good ankles and about treating bad ones.

A.T.'s Image, like his sire Native Dancer, had bad ankles.

Cavalaris first saw Fuller's promising Native Dancer colt in December 1966 at Bonnie Braes Farm near Ocala, Florida, where the strapping gray had been sent to begin his training. Cavalaris had been Fuller's trainer for about five years, hired on the recommendation of trainer Horatio Luro, who won the Kentucky Derby with Decidedly in 1962 and again with Northern Dancer in 1964.

Cavalaris had a division of his stable at Hialeah, and since the trainer was already in the neighborhood, Fuller asked the man's opinion about his yearlings. In the well-bred gray colt, he saw a good-looking, beautiful horse, but one that was fat and out of shape. It would take a lot of work to get him fit, Cavalaris thought, and that might present a problem.

The trainer did not like the look of the colt's ankles. It was the only fault the trainer could find, but it might be a serious one. The ankles were a bit enlarged, not the worst ankles Cavalaris had ever seen, but clearly not the best, either. The outline of the joints, the underlying bone structure, was not to Cavalaris's liking, especially in a horse that was just starting serious work.

Trainers obviously prefer sound horses to sore ones, and Cavalaris told Fuller about his concerns. Consider the potential problems of keeping a horse with questionable ankles sound, Cavalaris advised his boss, and if Fuller wanted to sell, then a fair price for the colt would be around $25,000.[7] By coincidence, Cavalaris's appraisal matched the amount of Fuller's investment for the breeding to Native Dancer and what he spent to claim Noors Image, with no room for profit. Add in the expenses of raising a horse for two years, and Cavalaris's appraisal would generate a net loss.

Fuller reluctantly entered the colt in a sale of horses in training in February 1967 over the objections of his wife, Joan, and despite his own serious misgivings about selling a horse he had named to honor his late father.

"I could not sell something I had named for my father," Fuller said. "But I had a trainer, a real good one, and he was giving me the best advice. So I was faced with a dilemma. Not only was I selling a colt I loved, but I was selling one named for my father. Somebody would buy it, race it, and it would be the one named for my father, who was a winner, losing."[8]

That problem was solved when the Jockey Club granted Fuller's request to change the colt's name to Dancer's Image. The other obstacle was more serious, and Fuller never really succeeded in convincing Joan Fuller, or himself, that selling the colt was a good idea.

Dancer's Image needed to bring a final bid of at least $35,000 to earn a decent return on Fuller's investment, but the bidding on Hip No. 37 stalled at $25,000. It was the figure Cavalaris thought would be a good price for the horse.

"Why do you want to sell him?" Joan Fuller kept asking as the auctioneer sought out another bid. "He's so beautiful." Without a good answer to his wife's question, Fuller upped the bid to $26,000. John Nerud, a future Hall of Fame trainer who knew his way around a good horse, was the bidder at $25,000, but he would go no further. For the amount of the sales company's commission on the transaction, Fuller bought back the Native Dancer colt he already owned. The next day, he turned Dancer's Image over to Cavalaris.

"I told Lou the colt was his baby now," Fuller recalled years later, "and that the rest was up to him."[9]

"Well, Peter," Cavalaris said, "we'll find out now for ourselves."[10]

***

Dancer's Image was so impressive during his morning workouts at Hialeah that Cavalaris made a bold and unconventional decision when he thought the colt was ready for his first start. Bypassing a race against other maidens, the typical proving ground for an unproven horse, Cavalaris shipped Dancer's Image to Arlington Park, northwest of Chicago, for his first start, a 5½-furlong allowance race on June 7, 1967.

Some owners might have vetoed Cavalaris's decision as too risky, but Fuller generally gave the trainer free rein about when and where to race the stable's horses. This was a change for Fuller, who for a time tried to micromanage his stable and who hired and fired trainers in rapid succession before Cavalaris came on board.

This was one occasion when some micromanaging might have been a good thing.

The trip to Chicago was a disaster.

Torrential rain turned the track into a quagmire that the inexperienced colt could not handle. He broke slowly and never got close to the leaders, eventually finishing seventh, sixteen lengths behind the winner. Like a golfer who cannot take a good game from the driving range to the course, Dancer's Image had been unable to duplicate his early morning form when it counted. Cavalaris started second guessing himself. The trainer was baffled—but not for long.

Dancer's Image came out of the Arlington Park race in good shape physically, and a cautiously optimistic Cavalaris ran him back just five days later at Woodbine in Canada. Dancer's Image started as the 2-5 favorite despite the dismal showing in Chicago, likely because of the colt's breeding and the sterling reputation Cavalaris had in his native Canada. He did not disappoint the Woodbine bettors. Running against other maidens this time out, he sprinted to the lead at the start and drew away over a fast track, winning the five-furlong race by eight lengths.

The loss in Chicago and the easy win in Canada were the first in a string of races that was both impressive for Dancer's Image and frustrating for Cavalaris. By the end of the year, the trainer had a Canadian champion two-year-old in his barn, but he still did not know with any confidence how good the colt really was. A winning racehorse is judged by the horses he defeats, and Dancer's Image was clearly the best two-year-old colt in Canada. He won every time he set foot on the race track at Woodbine, Fort Erie and Greenwood, seven wins in all, four of them in stakes races.

Outside Canada, though, Dancer's Image was more of a question mark. The colt ran second four times, but he could manage only one win in eight starts as a two-year-old in the United States. His lone victory came in November in the Maryland Futurity at Laurel Race Course when he held on to win by a nose over a largely undistinguished field of juveniles.

At the end of the season, Dancer's Image was one of six two-year-olds assigned 115 pounds on the Experimental Free Handicap. Vitriolic was the top weight with 126 pounds.

Fifteen starts in six months is a long, tough campaign, especially for a two-year-old with questionable ankles, but Dancer's Image seemed to handle it with few obvious problems. He went to the track most mornings, often for long gallops that built stamina without overly taxing his ankles; the training program appeared to work. Cavalaris treated the ankles with a variety of blisters, paints and liniment braces over the months, and when the ankles swelled, the trainer said the condition was an adverse reaction due to the tender skin that is common with gray horses. Ten years earlier, trainer Bill Winfrey told reporters the same thing when Native Dancer came up with puffy ankles.

Mostly, though, Cavalaris relied on cold water bandages and ice—lots of ice—to keep Dancer's Image sound. Nearly every day, the colt was walked with his forelegs swathed in bandages kept chilled with cold water, and he stood in a tub of ice for at least two hours before his races. Standing a horse in ice longer than that, Cavalaris thought, had no therapeutic benefit. In the stall, Dancer's Image always wore standing bandages over a light liniment, standard practice for all of the horses Cavalaris trained.

The colt's ankles had worried Cavalaris since the day he first saw them, but, against the odds, Dancer's Image had managed to stay racing sound through six hard months of racing. The ankles certainly were a problem worth keeping an eye on, but they were a problem that apparently could be managed with the proper care—so far, at least.

***

The Kentucky Derby, the Preakness Stakes and the Belmont Stakes compose the most demanding assignment a three-year-old Thoroughbred ever will face: three races run at varying distances, over three different tracks, in the short span of five weeks. In anticipation of the task ahead, trainers often decide to rest horses being pointed toward the classics, to give them some time off between their two-year-old and three-year-old seasons.

Cavalaris adopted a somewhat different strategy with Dancer's Image. The colt made his first start at three on a snowy New Year's Day at Laurel Race Course in Maryland, just twenty-three days after his last start as a two-year-old. The heavy favorite among the few bettors who braved the miserable weather, Dancer's Image had the lead in the stretch but he shied away from a piece of paper blowing across the track, stumbled badly and finished second. A few days later, Cavalaris shipped his horses south to Hialeah for the winter, and Dancer's Image got a well-deserved, if slightly delayed, holiday.

Six weeks in the warm Miami sun clearly agreed with Dancer's Image. The colt filled out, and he was looking better all the time. He trained well, impressing Cavalaris and the clockers, and his ankles seemed to be holding up. Cavalaris continued doing what had worked so far to keep Dancer's Image racing sound—the ice water bandages and tubs and tubs of ice—and he added daily doses of Azium powder in the colt's feed. Azium is a trade

Dancer's Image and trainer Lou Cavalaris Jr. *George Featherston photo. Courtesy of the* Thoroughbred Times.

name of dexamethasone, a catabolic steroid used to reduce inflammation, especially in joints.

One morning in February, Dancer's Image worked seven furlongs in 1:24⅖, and Cavalaris knew that the colt was ready for a race. Peter Fuller wanted to see his green and gold colors in the Heagerty Stakes, a late-February race restricted to Maryland-bred horses at Bowie Race Course, so Cavalaris shipped Dancer's Image north. He left the rest of his stable at Hialeah and began commuting from Florida to Maryland.

Dancer's Image won the seven-furlong Heagerty, coming from off the pace to win by a length, and then the colt followed up the win with two disappointing efforts in a pair of Bowie stakes, the 6-furlong Francis Scott Key Stakes and the 1⅛-mile Prince George's Stakes. The reversal in form left Cavalaris bewildered and wondering anew if Dancer's Image was a legitimate Derby horse. He and Fuller would get their answer a couple of weeks later in a prep race for the $100,000 added Governor's Gold Cup.

Dancer's Image had been most successful either setting the pace or running close to the leaders, but that was a running style that Cavalaris did not think would work in the longer races of the Triple Crown. The colt had run while wearing blinkers in all except one of his first nineteen starts, and as an experiment, Cavalaris took them off for a March 30 allowance race at Bowie. He thought the change in equipment would make it easier for a jockey to rate Dancer's Image, to keep him off the early pace in preparation for a run at the finish.

Cavalaris did not have a regular rider for Dancer's Image at two or early in his three-year-old season. The colt had been ridden by eight different jockeys, and he had won stakes for four of them, so settling on one rider did not seem to be a priority. Cavalaris was not committed to anyone in particular for the Governor's Gold Cup, and when he learned that Bobby Ussery was coming down from New York and might be available for the prep race, he jumped at the chance to retain the veteran rider.

Ussery had won the Kentucky Derby the previous year with Proud Clarion, a 30-1 long shot that rallied from off the pace, and that was exactly the kind of patient ride that Cavalaris wanted for Dancer's Image. The jockey was going to be at Bowie with a mount in the Barbara Fritchie Handicap anyway, and the jockey's agent signed on for the Gold Cup prep race that would be run a little earlier on the afternoon's card. Ussery had ridden for Cavalaris in the past, so the trainer was familiar with the rider's skill. Neither the agent nor Ussery knew that the mount was Dancer's Image, however, or that the allowance race was preparation for a $100,000 stakes race.

One of the disadvantages of running a large public stable with divisions at different tracks is that the trainer cannot be in two places at the same time. When there is a conflict, at least one owner is likely to feel slighted because the trainer is somewhere else, tending to someone else's horses. Cavalaris stayed in Florida and left Dancer's Image in the care of an assistant for the Gold Cup prep race. His instructions, relayed to Ussery by the assistant who saddled Dancer's Image for the absent Cavalaris, were simple: let the horse relax and make a run at the end.

Ussery did just as he was told.

He kept Dancer's Image eight lengths off the pace for a half mile and then hustled the colt through the stretch to win by a nose. Verbatim, a good horse whose owner also had Kentucky Derby ambitions, was second. Cavalaris and Fuller now had a better idea about how Dancer's Image would stack up against stakes-quality horses, and they started making serious Derby plans of their own. Ussery's horse finished out of the money in the Barbara Fritchie, the race that had brought him to Bowie in the first place, but the day was not a total loss for the jockey. He left Maryland with the mount on Dancer's Image, who was fast becoming a legitimate Derby contender.

Chapter 3

NO GOOD DEED GOES
UNPUNISHED

The 1960s were defined by violence.

Massive escalation of the war in Vietnam following the Bay of Tonkin incident was matched by a wave of political assassinations and growing civil unrest in the United States. The shooting of a fifteen-year-old African American youth by an off-duty white police officer touched off a riot in Harlem in 1964, and thirty-four people died during five days of rioting in Watts the next year. Things got even worse in 1967, when weeklong riots in Detroit and Newark left sixty-six people dead and hundreds injured.

On April 3, 1968, a Wednesday, the Reverend Martin Luther King Jr. left room 306 at the Lorraine Motel in Memphis for the Mason Temple, where he delivered his "I Have Been to the Mountaintop" speech before an enthusiastic crowd of supporters. A day later, the Reverend King was dead, gunned down by an assassin while the civil rights leader and Nobel Peace Prize winner stood on the second floor balcony of the motel. The killing touched off riots in more than one hundred cities, including Baltimore.

With the city in turmoil, a national day of mourning set for Sunday and the Reverend King's funeral scheduled for Monday, the Saturday card at Bowie Race Course thirty miles away was about the last thing on anybody's mind. There were suggestions that the $100,000 Governor's Gold Cup should be canceled or at least postponed, but track management ultimately decided to run the race as planned. There were no incidents at the track.

A good trainer knows about keeping good ankles sound and bad ankles from getting worse, and a good trainer knows not to change things that seem to be working. Lou Cavalaris kept Bobby Ussery in the saddle and the blinkers off Dancer's Image for the Gold Cup. That combination was successful the first time Ussery rode Dancer's Image, but the Gold Cup would be the first real test of Cavalaris's plan to try and get Dancer's Image to relax and conserve his speed early in a race. The Gold Cup would be run at 1 1/16 miles; the prep had been only 7 furlongs, a sprint distance that was not long enough to evaluate whether the come-from-behind strategy really worked.

Cavalaris was on hand for the Gold Cup, and once again, Ussery followed the trainer's instruction to the letter, allowing Dancer's Image to lag near the back of the fourteen-horse field during the early going. At one point, he was almost ten lengths behind the leaders. Ussery got Dancer's Image rolling on the final turn, and the gray colt charged down the stretch to win by three lengths. His time for the race, 1:42⅘, was just ⅕ of a second off the track record. It was an impressive performance, one clearly worth a trip to Churchill Downs for the Kentucky Derby, if Dancer's Image stayed sound. For this horse, that always was the question.

Cavalaris missed the prep race, but he worked a trip to Bowie for the Gold Cup into a hectic travel schedule. At the time, he had horses in training at Hialeah in Florida, in Toronto, at Bowie and in New York, where Dancer's Image would have his last Derby prep in the Wood Memorial Stakes. Cavalaris watched Dancer's Image cool out after the Gold Cup, and while the horse was not lame, the trainer did notice heat in the right front ankle. It was an on-again, off-again condition that Cavalaris attributed to almost two months of training and racing over the hard track at Bowie.

The trainer already was rubbing the colt's ankles and knees with Absorbine every morning, adding Azium powder to his feed each day, standing him in bandages at night and using cold water bandages and tubs of ice on a regular basis. Unless things got worse, Cavalaris did not think the ankle condition was serious enough to warrant more drastic measures. He was a successful trainer who knew not to change things that were working, not with the Kentucky Derby a month away.

***

The assassination of the Reverend King had a profound effect on Peter Fuller and tempered the excitement of Dancer's Image winning the Governor's Gold Cup. Both the Reverend King and his widow, Coretta, had attended Boston University, where Fuller was a trustee. He did not know the couple well, but he had met them when the Reverend King accepted an honorary degree from the school. He wanted to do something to honor the slain civil rights leader and, just maybe, to demonstrate to everyone that the gap between black and white Americans did not have to be filled with hate.

Before the Gold Cup Fuller discussed with his farm manager, Bob Casey, the idea of donating the winner's share of the purse, more than $60,000, to Mrs. King if Dancer's Image won the race. The colt did win, and a few days later, Fuller delivered a check to the Reverend King's widow in Atlanta. There seemed to be no ulterior motives or hidden agendas, just a sincere white man trying to help out in the best way he knew how.[11]

Fuller did not go out of his way to publicize the gift, but it also seemed wrong to try and keep it secret, as Mrs. King and some other prominent African Americans like Harry Belafonte urged.[12] Fuller sent out a press release after the Gold Cup, but it was ignored almost everywhere outside the trade press. The *Blood-Horse* magazine made note of Fuller's generosity in the caption of a winner's circle photograph, but the general public did not become aware of the gift to Mrs. King until the afternoon of the Wood Memorial. Television announcer Win Elliot had some dead air to fill during the broadcast of the race, and he mentioned the check.

Reaction to Fuller's act of generosity was mixed. There was sentiment in favor of the gift and against it, but that was to be expected. The civil rights movement had polarized the nation. What was more troubling were what Fuller called the "funny" letters. And by "funny," he did not mean humorous. Some of the letters were vicious, some were threatening, all were racist.

The criticism, especially from some other people in racing, might have surprised Fuller, but it probably should not have. The timing of the gift was not the best. The Reverend King and the Kentucky Derby had a history, and it was not a good one. Just a year earlier, civil rights protests, both real and threatened, had left Churchill Downs looking like an armed camp for the ninety-third running of the Kentucky Derby.

On April 11, 1967, the Louisville Board of Alderman voted down an open housing resolution, and demonstrators moved their protests to the streets. Comedian and activist Dick Gregory was on hand for the marches, and he threatened to disrupt the Derby: "I ain't going to lay down in front of a horse myself, but there's a lot of cats that will. If it comes to closing the Derby up, we'll just have to close it up." It was not an idle threat. Confrontations became more violent, the Derby Week's Pegasus Parade was canceled out of concern for the safety of spectators and participants and five young men managed to slip past Churchill Downs security and run onto the track during a race. No one was injured in the stunt, but the threat to the Derby appeared genuine. The Ku Klux Klan even offered to show up in hoods and robes to help provide security.[13] Thankfully, the offer was turned down.

A few days before the race, the Reverend King flew into Louisville to take an active role in the open housing demonstrations. In private, he was ambivalent about disrupting the Derby, but public perception was clear: the race, and with it a significant part of Louisville's identity, was in jeopardy, and the civil rights leader was at the forefront of the protest.[14]

Kentucky governor Edward T. Breathitt contacted the Reverend King and urged him to call off the planned demonstration. A sit-down strike in the middle of the track would put the young people at serious risk, Governor Breathitt said. He promised National Guardsmen, unarmed but trained to deal with protests, and state police to protect the marchers, but he said he could not guarantee their safety. Three hundred additional police officers, six hundred National Guard troops and an air police unit eventually were mustered for security duty at Churchill Downs.[15]

The Reverend King called Governor Breathitt at 11:00 a.m. on Derby Day.

"I thought about it Governor," the Reverend King said. "We're not going to have them there."[16] It was an act of good faith, the Reverend King explained. He left Louisville later that day. He returned during the summer and said that "our beloved nation is still a racist country" and that the "vast majority of white Americans are racist."[17]

It would be no surprise if Fuller's association with Mrs. King, and by extension the entire civil rights movement, rankled people in Louisville.

***

Dancer's Image walked under tack for three-quarters of an hour the day after the Gold Cup and then galloped the morning after that. This was standard practice for Cavalaris's horses following a race. When Dancer's Image jogged or galloped, he went the "wrong way" on the track, clockwise rather than counterclockwise, as he would for a serious workout or a race. Cavalaris did that with all the horses he trained. He thought that made horses easier to gallop on galloping days and more willing to breeze on days when they would be asked for speed.

No Good Deed Goes Unpunished

After Dancer's Image was shipped to Belmont Park on Long Island for the Wood Memorial, there was not a lot of training left for Cavalaris to do. The horse already was fit so he galloped most mornings, with a couple of faster works thrown in to keep him sharp on days when Cavalaris was in town. The trainer still was commuting from one track to another during the two weeks between the Gold Cup and the Wood Memorial, and he did not see the colt every day.

Dancer's Image always was the star of Peter Fuller's small stable, but for Cavalaris, the situation was different. Until Dancer's Image won impressively in the Governor's Gold Cup, he had been one of many promising horses in the trainer's far-flung stable. But now the Wood Memorial was two weeks away, the Kentucky Derby was two weeks after that and Dancer's Image was developing into a legitimate contender. Cavalaris was getting excited about the horse, and he paid closer attention to Dancer's Image before the Wood Memorial than ever before.

Dancer's Image showed no lameness before the Wood, but Cavalaris did notice some minor swelling in the colt's ankles. The heat that Cavalaris had found in the ankles still was there, but the condition was not serious enough to make Dancer's Image lame. The trainer crossed his fingers and did not change the therapy regimen that was keeping the colt sound enough to race.

The Wood was the last start for Dancer's Image prior to the Kentucky Derby, and it was significant in several ways. He would carry Derby weight of 126 pounds for the first time, it would be the longest distance he had run so far (1⅛ miles) and he would face the toughest field he ever had raced against. It was the colt's final test, and he passed with flying colors, rallying from far off the pace to win by three-quarters of a length. Iron Ruler and Verbatim, both legitimate Derby horses, finished second and third. The time was good, 1:49 for 1⅛ miles, and Dancer's Image was drawing away at the finish.

It was an impressive victory, more than good enough to warrant a trip to Churchill Downs if Fuller still entertained any doubts about that, but the win did not quiet all of the colt's critics. Wise Exchange, a promising distance horse that would have been one of the favorites, was a last-minute scratch, and the jockey on Iron Ruler came in for some criticism for a possibly premature move to the lead. Iron Ruler was in front by four lengths before Dancer's Image ran past him in the stretch, and who knows what would have happened with a more prudent ride on the second-place horse.

If he stayed sound, Dancer's Image would be the first starter in the Kentucky Derby for both Fuller and Cavalaris. The trainer had come close the year before with Canadian champion Cool Reception, which ran third

Dancer's Image and exercise rider Ernie Warne. *Winants Brothers photo. Courtesy of the* Blood-Horse.

in the Derby Trial on the Tuesday before the Derby. Cavalaris thought Cool Reception was a lock to finish among the top three in the Kentucky Derby, good incentive to run, but he decided to pass anyway because he thought a second hard race in five days would be too taxing on the horse. He was planning for the long run, but things did not work out. Five weeks later, Cool Reception ran second to Damascus in the Belmont Stakes but fractured a leg in the process and never raced again.

Looking ahead to the Derby and possibly the Triple Crown, Dancer's Image faced two major obstacles: his ankles and a Calumet Farm powerhouse named Forward Pass. Forward Pass had won the Florida Derby in March and would win the Blue Grass Stakes a few days after the Wood. The colt was Calumet's most promising Derby contender in several years, and the prospect of an eighth Derby trophy for the storied central Kentucky farm was attractive to a lot of people.

Chapter 4

THE DERBY DOC

Peter Fuller spent a lot of time on the phone during the weeks leading up to the Kentucky Derby. When it became clear that Dancer's Image was headed for Churchill Downs, there were airplane reservations to make, hotel rooms to secure and Derby tickets to negotiate. Fuller was extremely confident about Dancer's Image, and his excitement was contagious. He wanted to share the experience with as many people as possible.

Counting family, friends and business associates, Fuller needed at least sixty tickets for race day, maybe more. It was a request well above the usual allotment set aside for owners of Derby horses and many more tickets than Churchill Downs president Wathen Knebelkamp was inclined to dole out, at least not without some serious haggling. It was like driving up to Fort Knox and asking for a few bars of gold from the repository, except that talking the soldiers out of the gold might have been easier.

Fuller made at least two telephone calls to Warner L. Jones Jr., a friend who owned Hermitage Farm in Goshen, a small town a few miles from Louisville. Jones was a prominent owner and breeder who also happened to be chairman of the Board of Churchill Downs, and Fuller needed some advice about a couple of important matters.

One call involved security for Dancer's Image after the horse arrived in Louisville. Most of the obnoxious letters Fuller received in the wake of the Governor's Gold Cup probably were written by crackpots, but it would be foolish to totally ignore the threats. Fuller said he was thinking about bringing some people down from the "homeland" for added protection, but

Jones told him that would not be a good idea.[18] "We've got great security," Jones said. He was adamant about it, and Fuller acquiesced.

Fuller also needed a reference from Jones for a good veterinarian to attend to Dancer's Image in Kentucky. Jones suggested Dr. Alex Harthill, a Jekyll-and-Hyde figure well known on the backstretch as a supremely gifted veterinarian but also as someone who, more often than not, moved around under a dark cloud of controversy. Fuller did not know Dr. Harthill, but relying on Jones's recommendation, he said "fine."[19] Dr. Harthill agreed because Odie Clellan, a longtime friend who had trained some horses for Fuller in New England, asked him to help.

Dr. Harthill met the plane carrying Dancer's Image when the colt arrived in Louisville on April 25, the Thursday after the Wood Memorial, and he helped get the horse settled into his stall in Barn 24 at Churchill Downs. Dancer's Image was lodged in Stall 7, the same stall occupied the previous year by Damascus, which was named Horse of the Year despite running one of the worst races of his career and finishing third in the Derby. Iron Ruler, which finished second to Dancer's Image in the Wood Memorial, also was housed in Barn 24.

Everyone on the backstretch called it the "Harthill Barn" because Barn 24 was the base of operations for the veterinarian's practice. Dancer's Image and Iron Ruler were not the first Derby horses to be housed in Barn 24. Dr. Harthill had a reputation for treating Kentucky Derby runners, and horses shipping in for the race from other tracks often occupied stalls in the Harthill Barn.

Other veterinarians who practiced on the backstretch worked out of their vehicles, but Dr. Harthill was an exception. It was an odd arrangement, allowing a veterinarian to have an office in the stable area, and one fraught with potential problems. Dr. Harthill was the only veterinarian granted the privilege, and there was some confusion over how it all came about. He moved into Barn 24 during the mid-1950s as his racetrack practice grew, eventually acquiring what amounted to squatters' rights. There never was a formal agreement between Churchill Downs and Dr. Harthill, and the veterinarian paid no rent for his use of the barn.[20]

It was not a surprise that Warner Jones recommended Dr. Harthill to Fuller. The two men had known each other for years, and the veterinarian often had treated horses at Jones's Hermitage Farm. It was there in the spring of 1949 that Dr. Harthill, not too long out of vet school, was called to treat a mare named Isolde. The mare was in serious trouble. Her foal was dead and positioned in such a way that it could not be delivered normally. Isolde was a very well-bred broodmare that Jones did not want to lose, but two other veterinarians had given up and her prospects for survival were grim.

The Derby Doc

Working inside Isolde with a device called a Bennsch saw, a thin and flexible piece of wire with razor-sharp teeth, Dr. Harthill methodically dismembered the dead foal. The gruesome procedure took hours to complete, and it exhausted Dr. Harthill, but the young veterinarian's heroic efforts saved the mare's life. Isolde recovered quickly, and later in the year, she was healthy enough to be bred to the stallion Royal Gem. From that breeding, Isolde produced Dark Star, winner of the 1953 Kentucky Derby and the only horse to defeat Native Dancer, sire of Dancer's Image.

***

If anyone ever was born to be a veterinarian, it was Alex Harthill. His father and grandfather maintained veterinary practices in Louisville, and his great-grandfather had been a veterinarian in Scotland during the nineteenth century. He started college the day after he finished prep school, and he started work almost immediately after he graduated from Ohio State University in March 1948 with a degree in veterinary medicine.

Finding clients can be a struggle for many new graduates, but Dr. Harthill had connections in the stratosphere of Thoroughbred racing. Hall of Fame trainers Ben Jones and Jimmy Jones, a father and son team that sent out a succession of champions and Triple Crown winners for Calumet Farm, were friends of Dr. Harthill's father, and the new graduate quickly swapped the halls of academia for the Calumet shed row. One of the first horses he took care of was Citation, winner of the Triple Crown a few months after Dr. Harthill graduated.

The "Derby Doc," veterinarian Alex Harthill. *Winants Brothers photo. Courtesy of the* Blood-Horse.

That same spring, Dr. Harthill saved the life of Ponder, a Calumet two-year-old colt that had been stabbed in the chest with a pitchfork. A serious infection set in, and for days, it was not clear that Ponder would even survive, let alone race. He did both, winning the Kentucky Derby the next year. Ponder was the son of a Derby winner (Pensive) who also sired a winner (Needles).

Word about this young veterinarian with extraordinary skills spread quickly, and soon his name was linked with one good horse after another.

Dr. Harthill's ascension from just another race track veterinarian to the "Derby Doc" was up and running. By the time Warner Jones recommended him to Fuller, Dr. Harthill had treated a succession of Kentucky Derby winners: Hill Gail, Dark Star, Swaps, Iron Liege, Tim Tam, Carry Back, Decidedly, Northern Dancer, Lucky Debonair and Proud Clarion.

Dr. Harthill's qualifications to treat another Derby contender never were in question, and for that Fuller was lucky to have him on board.

That was the good news.

The bad news was a reputation for chicanery that dogged Dr. Harthill almost from the start.[21]

In 1954, Texas oilman Sam E. Wilson Jr. complained to the FBI following a race won by one of the owner's horses at Hawthorne in Chicago. Wilson said that Dr. Harthill told him that he had fixed the race, and that Wilson owed him $1,500. Wilson later recanted. The $1,500 actually had been a commission on the sale of some horses, he said, and the FBI investigation was dropped.

Dr. Harthill came under scrutiny again later that year, after the winner of a race at Keeneland Race Course in Kentucky tested positive for a prohibited stimulant. A groom testified that Dr. Harthill had injected the horse with something prior to the race, but the veterinarian denied any wrongdoing. He said the shots were koagamin and vitamin K, medications often used for horses that bled during a race. The trainer and groom were handed sixty-day suspensions by the Kentucky State Racing Commission, but Dr. Harthill was not disciplined.

Still, later in 1954, Dr. Harthill was suspended for sixty days by the Illinois Racing Board after a horse named Mr. Black tested positive for a prohibited stimulant. Mr. Black won the Grassland Handicap at Washington Park three days after he was given a medication containing a stimulant by Dr. Harthill. The suspension was not directly related to the treatment, which Harthill admitted, but rather was based on his failure to notify the commission veterinarian, Mr. Black's trainer, the assistant trainer or apparently anyone else that he had administered a stimulant a few days before the race. Mr.

Black presumably could have been scratched from the Grassland Handicap if the trainer had known about the treatment.

Dr. Harthill took the Illinois Racing Board to court, and a judge granted a stay of the suspension to "a man of Harthill's stature pending a full hearing later." There apparently were no hard feelings. When Dr. Harthill applied for a license to practice at Illinois tracks three years later, the racing board granted the request.

Authorities in Louisiana claimed that Dr. Harthill was involved in a multihorse drugging and bribery scheme at the Fair Grounds in 1955, but he was acquitted on all charges by a five-person jury. The Louisiana State Racing Commission restored Dr. Harthill to good standing after the verdict.

The investigations continued, at Keeneland, at Churchill Downs, at Oaklawn Park, but suspicion and innuendo never gave way to any hard evidence of wrongdoing. Dr. Harthill shrugged off the rumors about his misdeeds as ingenious tall tales fueled by professional jealousy and hostile reporters, and his supporters—there were many—probably agreed. Success solves a lot of problems, and Dr. Harthill was successful.

***

Neither Lou Cavalaris nor assistant trainer Robert Barnard accompanied Dancer's Image to Louisville when the horse was shipped from New York to Louisville. The horse's groom, Russell Parchen, made the trip. Cavalaris arrived at Churchill Downs on Saturday, two days after Dancer's Image had taken up residence in Barn 24 and two days before Barnard arrived. When he got to the Harthill Barn, Cavalaris was dismayed to learn that the horse had wrenched his right front ankle. Dancer's Image galloped early on Saturday morning, and that workout might have been the source of the injury. Or there was another more likely possibility: Dancer's Image was a big, strong and rambunctious horse, and he had acted up while being grazed on Saturday. Odds were good that he twisted the ankle rearing and lunging at the end of a lead shank.

Cavalaris and Dr. Harthill conferred under the shed row on Sunday morning, debating what to do. The ankle was hot and swollen, but X-rays taken by the veterinarian that morning revealed no damage to the joint itself. Under other circumstances, rest might have been the treatment of choice, but that was not an option with the Derby a week away. Dr. Harthill suggested

Dancer's Image and trainer Lou Cavalaris Jr. *George Featherston photo. Courtesy of the* Thoroughbred Times.

to Cavalaris that a dose of Butazolidin might be a quick fix to help reduce the inflammation. The trainer concurred. Around 10:30 a.m., a four-gram bolus of the drug was administered to Dancer's Image with a balling gun, a long-handled device with a sliding plunger used to force pills down a horse's throat.

Butazolidin—"Bute" in the lexicon of veterinarians and horsemen—is a trade name for the drug phenylbutazone. It is a potent analgesic with anti-inflammatory properties similar to aspirin. It was first synthesized in 1946 for human use, and by the early 1950s, the drug had gained wide acceptance among veterinarians. Bute enjoys a peculiar place among racetrack medications. It is neither a stimulant nor a depressant—the types of drugs most often associated with nefarious dealings and fixed horse races. Instead, Bute simply allows a horse to perform up to the animal's full potential by relieving pain and swelling.

Manipulating the odds in a series of races to win a bet still is possible, of course. Bettors rely on a horse's past performances to predict how well a horse will perform in an upcoming race. Run a chronically sore horse in a race without Bute, and he is likely to perform poorly, which means higher odds when he runs again. Add a dose of Bute for that next race, and the horse might win at artificially long odds. Bettors call it an overlay when a horse starts at longer-than-expected odds. When Bute is involved, it also sounds a lot like cheating.

The drug had an obvious image problem. Chemical properties aside, to the public, Bute was dope.

State racing commissions began testing for phenylbutazone in the late 1950s, and by 1962, use of the drug was controlled everywhere. Kentucky was the last state to ban the drug for racing, and officials there did so reluctantly and only to promote a uniform medication rule. No horse in the state had been disqualified for a Bute positive since testing started.[22]

Most states, Kentucky included, initially adopted a "zero tolerance" policy that allowed Bute to be used while a horse was training but prohibited a horse from racing with any trace of the medication in its system. That might sound hypocritical, but it was a pragmatic policy that recognized two things: Bute had tremendous value as a therapeutic medication for a horse during the rigors of training and testing for the drug in a nonrace environment was impractical.

Cavalaris had used Bute on his horses in the past, but never before on Dancer's Image. The trainer thought the drug could help a horse with an injury or one that was sore, but he did not use it routinely for training. He thought it was unfair to train a horse on Bute when the drug could not be used for racing.

It all came down to timing.

Zero tolerance created a serious problem for veterinarians and trainers because the analgesic effect of Bute on an injury faded well before all traces of the drug vanished from a horse's system. As a result, a horse could test positive for Bute even though there no longer was any therapeutic effect from the drug to affect performance. The generally accepted clearance time for a dose of the medication was a maximum of seventy-two hours, three days, but that was an educated guess at best. Neither Cavalaris nor Dr. Harthill was a chemist, and the actual clearance time could vary greatly depending on the dosage and the horse.

They were not overly concerned about the four grams of Bute administered to Dancer's Image on Sunday because of the timing of the dose. If Dancer's Image won the Derby—and Cavalaris thought he would win—it was highly unlikely that the drug would show up in a postrace test. It was a gamble of sorts, but a necessary one under the circumstances. The Derby still was six days away, and that should allow plenty of time for the Bute to clear the colt's system.

The Sunday dose of Bute did mean a change of plans for Dancer's Image, though. Fuller and Cavalaris had been leaning toward running Dancer's Image in the Derby Trial on Tuesday as a final prep race, but now those plans would have to be scrapped. Cavalaris knew that two days was too short a time to be certain that traces of Bute would not taint a winner's drug test.

Derby Week was starting on a sour note for Fuller, for Cavalaris and for Dancer's Image.

Chapter 5

THE MOST EXCITING TWO
MINUTES IN SPORTS

When Lou Cavalaris arrived at Barn 24 early Monday morning and looked in on Dancer's Image, he was pleased to find the heat and swelling mostly gone from the horse's right front ankle. The Bute apparently had done its job, but there was an unexpected side effect. It also made Dancer's Image sick. The horse had diarrhea, and he was showing some signs of colic. Cavalaris decided against medicating Dancer's Image for the diarrhea and the colic, which were not severe, and after an hour or so, the horse was in good enough shape to go to the track. He worked three furlongs in :36—a solid 12 seconds/furlong pace, not too fast, not too slow—and the New England Derby Train seemed to be back on track.

Satisfied by the way Dancer's Image cooled out after the workout, Cavalaris left the track for Standiford Field to catch a plane to Detroit where he had a division of his public stable. He was back at Churchill Downs early on Tuesday morning to watch exercise rider Ernie Warne take Dancer's Image out for an easy three-mile gallop. Cavalaris told reporters that he was "delighted" with the workout, and that he planned one final three-furlong "blowout" for the horse on Friday. The trainer was back in the air again later that day on a flight to Fort Erie in Canada where he had several horses running on Wednesday and Thursday.

With fifty horses in training for a dozen owners at several different tracks, Cavalaris was an absentee trainer by necessity, even for a race as important as the Kentucky Derby. He flew in on days when Dancer's Image had serious workouts scheduled but often left the colt in the care of others when he had horses racing elsewhere. Day-to-day responsibility for Dancer's Image fell to assistant trainer Robert Barnard and groom Russell Parchen. Barnard started with Cavalaris in October 1967, working his way up from a groom to foreman and assistant trainer. He did not do a lot of actual training in Kentucky, though. Mostly, Barnard just followed the instructions left for Dancer's Image by Cavalaris. He followed them to the letter.

Oddly, especially considering the amount of time Cavalaris was away from Churchill Downs and the responsibility given to Barnard, there was not a lot of communication between the two men. Barnard arrived at Churchill Downs on Monday before the Derby, and although Cavalaris left detailed instructions about the scheduled workouts for Dancer's Image, the trainer neglected to tell his assistant about the dose of Bute the horse received the day before.[23]

While Barnard substituted for Cavalaris at Barn 24, Peter Fuller was forced into a stand-in role for the absent trainer at social functions throughout the week. On Tuesday evening at the Kentucky Thoroughbred Breeders Association Trainers' Dinner, Fuller recalled how he entered Dancer's Image in a sale for two-year-olds in Florida and then bought him back at his wife's urging. Dancer's Image was the "best horse he ever had," a confident Fuller said.

Earlier that day, Fuller was sitting in Ed McGrath's clubhouse box watching the races. McGrath was a Louisville insurance agent who had brokered a $1.5 million mortality policy for Dancer's Image, a tenfold increase in the coverage Fuller had on the colt just two months earlier.

"Ed," Fuller said, "let's take a dry run right now on the shortest way from here down to the tunnel leading to the track and the winner's circle. I sure didn't bring Dancer's Image all the way to Louisville just to see my colors out there. I came to win this race and I've never been so confident."[24]

Not every horse comes to Churchill Downs with a legitimate chance to win. For some owners, the ones who just want to see their colors in the post parade, the prestige of having a runner in the Derby is incentive enough. And $1,600 ($100 to nominate, $500 to enter, $1,000 to start) is a cheap price for prime Derby tickets that might cost ten times that amount from a scalper. Fuller was not one of those status seekers. His first Derby horse was a good one, and mapping out the quickest route to the winner's circle was more than wishful thinking.

The clubhouse and grandstand at Churchill Downs are designed to accommodate the huge throngs of people that show up on Derby Day. On most afternoons, though, the whole place looks deserted. Most of the betting windows are closed; voices and footsteps echo off the cavernous walls. The circuitous route from owner's box to winner's circle was a cinch to navigate on a Tuesday afternoon, when only 10,500 people were in the stands.

The going would be tougher on Saturday, with people packed shoulder to shoulder, if Dancer's Image won.

All the trainers at the dinner, and Fuller too, despite his confidence, agreed that Forward Pass would start as the favorite in the Derby. Henry Forrest, who trained Forward Pass for Calumet Farm, said that the Churchill Downs race track was fast and getting faster, and he predicted a winning time of "two minutes or less."[25] A two-minute trip over the Derby's 1¼ miles would equal the record set by Northern Dancer in 1964, and coming from someone else, Forrest's prediction might have sounded like a number snatched out of thin air. But Forrest had reason to be optimistic.

Around three o'clock on a mild and sunny Tuesday afternoon, Forrest had Forward Pass on the track for a workout between the fourth and fifth races. Most training is done in the morning, not between races later in the day, but Forrest had done the same thing with Kauai King in 1966, and that horse went on to win the Derby. Like Dancer's Image, Kauai King was sired by Native Dancer. He was the stallion's first Kentucky Derby winner. Fuller and Cavalaris were counting on Dancer's Image to be the sire's second.

Exercise rider Joe Swart took Forward Pass from the barn to the saddling paddock, where Forrest gave jockey Ismael Valenzuela a leg up on the colt. Valenzuela was not the regular rider for Forward Pass. He had been a last-minute replacement for Don Brumfield, who came down with a case of food poisoning prior to the Blue Grass Stakes at Keeneland Race Course the week before the Derby. Forward Pass led all the way and won the Blue Grass by five lengths, establishing himself as the clear favorite for the Derby.

Now Forrest had a serious problem. Brumfield had won five races as the regular rider for Forward Pass, but Valenzuela clearly got along well with the horse. Plus there was sentiment and some history on Valenzuela's side. Ten years earlier, substituting for an injured Bill Hartack, Valenzuela won Calumet's seventh Derby with Tim Tam. There was pressure from his employer for Forrest to drop Brumfield and keep Valenzuela on Forward Pass for the Derby, and the trainer acquiesced.

Brumfield took himself off the horse, publicly blaming some lingering aftereffects from the bad chicken salad that had sidelined him before the Blue Grass Stakes, and Valenzuela got the mount. After the decision to replace Brumfield with Valenzuela, Mrs. Gene Markey, owner of Calumet Farm, promised to pay both riders the standard 10 percent commission if her horse won.[26] Brumfield, who had ridden Forward Pass in all but two of his previous races, wound up watching the Derby on television at his home near Nicholasville, Kentucky.

Forrest expected Forward Pass to work a mile in 1:39 or so on Tuesday afternoon, but the muscular, chestnut colt surprised everyone. He was clocked in 1:37 for a mile and then galloped out another furlong for a final time of 1:51⅓. The time earned a round of applause from the fifteen thousand spectators on hand and praise from Valenzuela: "He really wanted to run."[27] It was the last serious workout for the consensus Derby favorite.

***

Exercise rider Ernie Warne was up on Dancer's Image again on Wednesday morning. The colt galloped 1½ miles, schooled in the paddock for about ten minutes and then galloped another 2½ miles before returning to the Harthill Barn. There was no indication that the right front ankle was bothering him at all.

Dancer's Image and exercise rider Ernie Warne. *Winants Brothers photo. Courtesy of the* Blood-Horse.

Fuller spent the day in Lexington scouting out Bluegrass farms where Dancer's Image might stand at stud following his retirement. The horse's value as a breeding stallion had increased exponentially from the Governor's Gold Cup through the Wood Memorial, and a win in the Derby almost certainly would lead to a high-priced syndication. One of the figures being bandied about was $3,000,000. If that happened, Dancer's Image would become only the twenty-eighth Thoroughbred syndicated for $1,000,000 or more. One of them was Kauai King, syndicated for $2,160,000 after he won the Derby, so a similar value—or more—for another classic-winning son of Native Dancer was not unreasonable. If Dancer's Image managed the rare feat of sweeping the Triple Crown, which no horse had accomplished since Calumet's Citation in 1948, his value at stud would skyrocket.

Serious money was riding on an iffy ankle that was about to blow up.

***

Peter Fuller still was standing in for Lou Cavalaris on Thursday morning when he showed up at the office of Churchill Downs racing secretary and handicapper Allan W. Lavin for the post position draw. Doc Lavin's office was too small for the large crowd crammed inside. There barely was enough room for the television cameras and hot lights, the reporters, a batch of trainers and Fuller. Post positions for the Derby were assigned through a double-blind draw. Eddie Yowell, trainer of Iron Ruler, one of the early favorites, pulled a slip of paper with a horse's name printed on it from a stack Lavin held in his hand. At the same time, Jim Conway, who conditioned long shot Francie's Hat, shook a numbered pill from a cup.

"Number 12," Conway said.

"Number 12 is Dancer's Image," Lavin read from the slip drawn by Yowell.

No problem there, Fuller said. Dancer's Image liked to come from behind with a strong run late in a race, and Ussery could take his time moving the horse from one of the outside post positions over to the rail. Dancer's Image would be last or close to it the first time past the grandstand anyway, so his post position did not matter very much.

"Number 13," Conway called out a few horses later.

"Number 13 is Forward Pass," Lavin said.

An outside post position might be more of a concern for Forward Pass. The Calumet colt did his best running while setting the pace and never had won from an outside post position. To get to an early lead, Milo Valenzuela would have to hustle his mount to the rail through a cavalry charge of horses vying for a good position after the start.

From the 18,846 Thoroughbreds foaled in 1965, a near-record 191 horses were nominated for the 1968 Kentucky Derby. Of those three-year-olds, just 14 were good enough and lucky enough to have a spot in the starting gate:

Post Position	Horse
1.	Iron Ruler
2.	T.V. Commercial
3.	Jig Time
4.	Kentucky Sherry
5.	Trouble Brewing
6.	Te Vega
7.	Don B.
8.	Verbatim
9.	Captain's Gig
10.	Francie's Hat
11.	Proper Proof
12.	Dancer's Image
13.	Forward Pass
14.	Gleaming Sword

***

Cavalaris left instructions for Dancer's Image to be galloped several miles on Thursday morning, just as the horse had done on Tuesday and Wednesday, but the troublesome right front ankle was acting up again. The joint was swollen and inflamed, as bad as it ever had been, but there was no pain when Robert Barnard flexed the joint.[28] Dr. Harthill had been monitoring Dancer's Image throughout the week, and he thought the ankle looked terrible. He advised against working the horse, but Bernard was reluctant to alter the training plan left by his boss.

Along with the workout schedule, Cavalaris left word that he was just a phone call away in Canada if the assistant needed anything or if there were any problems with Dancer's Image. He could be reached at the track in the morning, the trainer said, or at his motel room any other time. Finding one of the favorites for the Kentucky Derby with a bad ankle two days before the race sounded important enough to get in touch with the man in charge, but Barnard did not make the call.[29] He simply insisted that Dancer's Image would be galloped as planned, no matter what Dr. Harthill or anyone else thought. This was not as unusual as it sounds. Cavalaris gave his assistants wide latitude to make decisions in his absence.[30] Cavalaris did not learn of the recurring ankle problem until he returned to the Harthill Barn on Friday.[31]

Dr. Harthill injected Dancer's Image with 20 cc of Azium, what he called a "massive dose" of the drug, and the colt went out for several easy trips around the Churchill Downs track with exercise rider Ernie Warne in the saddle. Dr. Harthill watched Dancer's Image work and was surprised to see that the horse's ankle looked better after the exercise than it had earlier in the morning. The horse stood in ice for a couple of hours after he worked, and by the afternoon, the ankle looked even better. Dr. Harthill attributed the rapid improvement to the exercise, to the Azium and to the iron constitution of Dancer's Image.[32]

The ankle was better still on Friday morning. Dancer's Image received a more normal dose of Azium, 6 cc this time, and injections of vitamin B complex, vitamin B12 and vitamin C. In his final serious workout, the horse breezed three furlongs in :37 flat, one of the fastest times of the day for Derby horses. Only T.V. Commercial was faster, going three furlongs in :36.

"He looks fine," Cavalaris said later in an impromptu press conference, "but we'll know more tonight. In the past, at times, his right front ankle has swollen to some extent and then gone down. He'll stand in ice, will be done up in liniment for the night. We'll gallop him tomorrow morning and if he isn't right, we won't run him. He's too nice a horse for that. But I think he's going to be all right. I am optimistic."[33]

There was no pressure from Fuller to run Dancer's Image if the colt was not sound. He told Cavalaris: "If there should be any problem, and if for any reason, bad luck or otherwise, this horse is not ready to run his race, you just forget about it, because that's the way it has to be."

"Why do you say that to me now," the trainer replied, "when we've had that understanding all the time that I have ever trained for you…So there can't be any other way."[34]

Dr. Harthill saw continued improvement in the ankle after the workout and again later in the afternoon. Another set of X-rays did nothing to dispel Cavalaris's optimism. Neither did a final gallop on Saturday morning.

"I've been up since 5:30," Cavalaris told reporters.

I couldn't sleep. Naturally I've been concerned about Dancer's Image's ankle. It's something he's had all his life, but this time he is coming up to the Kentucky Derby. Fortunately, he had a good, strong gallop this morning and the ankle is fine. We will have no excuses on that score. He won't be short, either. I promise you. He's had his work this week even though there was a risk of aggravating the ankle.

I've been trying to find the slightest excuse to scratch this horse. Honestly, I wouldn't want to run him unless he was absolutely all right. But he seems to be all right and so we are going to run him.[35]

The only question remaining was whether to give Dancer's Image a final injection of Azium on Saturday. It was legal in Kentucky, and might have been insurance against a sore ankle, but Cavalaris decided against it after the Friday workout. He told the veterinarian of his decision on Saturday morning.

"That's fine," Dr. Harthill said. "The ankle looks beautiful."[36]

***

The clubhouse and grandstand at Churchill Downs easily accommodated the crowd of more than 100,000 people who turned out in perfect weather on Derby Day. The paddock where the entries were saddled prior to the race, on the other hand, was woefully inadequate for the 14 horses, trainers, jockeys, owners, celebrities and other assorted hangers-on. Plans to enlarge the paddock had been on the drawing board for a while, but for the 1968 Derby, the saddling area was packed.

The sixth race went off at three-thirty in the afternoon, and then there was a one-hour break before the Derby. This was longer than the usual half hour scheduled between races on ordinary days. The extra time was built into the Derby Day schedule so bettors fighting crowds at the pari-mutuel windows would not get shutout. More than $2.35 million, a record, would be wagered on the Derby. It takes some time for that much money to change hands at the betting windows.

A few minutes after the horses from the sixth race cleared the track, activity picked up in the barns, and the procession of Derby horses started. It takes

Dancer's Image and jockey Bobby Ussery in the post parade before the Kentucky Derby. *Winants Brothers photo. Courtesy of the* Blood-Horse.

less than fifteen minutes to walk from Barn 24 to the paddock, so there was no particular hurry. Most trainers like to have their horses arrive at the last minute so they do not have to stand around in the paddock any longer than necessary, but Forward Pass was one of the first to arrive. When Dancer's Image walked to the paddock, the colt was wearing a light blanket and all four legs were swathed in the cold water bandages that Cavalaris favored. The horse looked sound and ready to run, but so did Forward Pass.

In the paddock, an official from the Kentucky State Racing Commission pushed his way through the crowd looking for Cavalaris. Preoccupied with getting Dancer's Image to the race in one piece, and possibly distracted by his trips out of town, he had never gotten around to filing an application for a Kentucky trainer's license. It was a technicality but an important one that had to be remedied before the race. The commission man signed Cavalaris up on the spot, and the problem was solved. The trainer tossed Bobby Ussery up onto the saddle, and the horses filed out to the track for the post parade and the traditional singing of "My Old Kentucky Home."

Drifting lazily over the track was the CBS blimp. It was the first time an airship like it had been used as a television camera platform for a Kentucky Derby broadcast.

Forward Pass was the 2-1 favorite, as everyone at the trainers' dinner predicted; Dancer's Image was the second choice at odds of 7-2.

The Most Exciting Two Minutes in Sports

***

The horses began loading into the starting gate at four-forty in the afternoon, and a half-minute later, veteran starter Jim Thomson sent them off. On the inside, jockey Jimmy Combest made a very aggressive move on Kentucky Sherry and sent the 15-1 long shot to the front. On the outside, Gleaming Sword swerved left as the starting gates opened and slammed into Forward Pass, which ran into Dancer's Image. The chain reaction hurt Forward Pass and helped Dancer's Image. Forward Pass was knocked off stride for a second or two by the collision, and Milo Valenzuela was hard pressed to get the Calumet colt across the track and up near the leaders on the rail. Ussery, on the other hand, was in no hurry, and he settled Dancer's Image into last place, eighteen or nineteen lengths behind the blistering pace being set by Kentucky Sherry.

Henry Forrest was livid over the ride Forward Pass was getting from Valenzuela, who was alternately hitting the colt, taking him back and then whipping him again to get within striking distance of Kentucky Sherry.

Dancer's Image trailed the field the first time past the stands. *Winants Brothers photo. Courtesy of the* Blood-Horse.

Dancer's Image still was far off the pace on the backstretch. *Winants Brothers photo. Courtesy of the* Blood-Horse.

Dancer's Image was exactly where Cavalaris, Fuller and Ussery wanted him to be, bringing up the rear the first time by the stands. Fuller must have wondered what his many guests were thinking, though, unaccustomed as they were to seeing the colt's heart-stopping stretch runs from last to first.

People watching the race on television had no idea how far back Dancer's Image actually was. The gap between the leaders and Fuller's colt grew so large that the grandstand cameras sometimes could not fit the entire field into one shot. Dancer's Image at times vanished into an electronic no man's land off the right side of the screen as the cameramen focused their attention on the front runners.

Kentucky Sherry sprinted the first quarter-mile in :22⅕, a half mile in :45⅘ and six furlongs in 1:09⅘. The early fractions were among the fastest ever in the Derby, the colt's time for six furlongs only ⅗ of a second off the track record for the distance. Early speed is impressive, but there was almost no chance that Kentucky Sherry could maintain that pace for 1¼ miles. He still was in front after a mile, but he was a tired horse, and Forward Pass was

Dancer's Image was in third place and gaining on the leaders at the top of the stretch. *Winants Brothers photo. Courtesy of the* Blood-Horse.

closing. The Calumet horse got the lead at the head of the stretch but it was short lived.

Captain's Gig pressed Kentucky Sherry during the early going, but he was ready to quit after a mile. Tired horses often bear out, and Captain's Gig did just that, drifting away from the rail at the head of the stretch. Getting to the lead with a come-from-behind horse like Dancer's Image often requires a healthy dose of good luck, and this was a monumental break for Ussery. He had been moving Dancer's Image up from last place, weaving between horses on the turn, and when the gap opened up on the rail, he jumped on the opportunity.

"There was a hole along the rail which was plenty big enough to get through," Ussery said, "and we just took off."[37] He hit Dancer's Image right handed a couple of times, and the colt surged to the lead. He dropped his whip, but it did not matter. There was no way that Forward Pass was going to outrun Dancer's Image that day.

"I saw Ussery coming up on the inside of me," Valenzuela said afterward, "but there was nothing I could do about it."[38]

Above: Dancer's Image drew clear near the finish, with Calumet farm's Forward Pass second. *Winants Brothers photo. Courtesy of the* Blood-Horse.

Left: The winning margin was 1½ lengths. *Winants Brothers photo. Courtesy of the* Blood-Horse.

Dancer's Image crossed the finish line 1½ lengths ahead of Forward Pass. Francie's Hat, at 33-1, was third. The winning time, an unspectacular 2:02⅕, was far off Henry Forrest's prediction and not even close to Northern Dancer's record of 2:00. But on May 4, 1968, it was fast enough.

An outrider caught up with Ussery and Dancer's Image on the backstretch and led them back to the winner's circle, as the also-rans returned to the barns. Ussery pulled off his helmet and waved it at the cheering crowd, as Fuller and his entourage retraced the owner's earlier dry run from the owners' section near the finish line through the stands and across the track.

"It's just great!" Fuller said in the winner's circle. "You couldn't dream it! Just look at all those wonderful people waving and applauding. Hey, Lou, you're just great, too. It's just wonderful. It's just wonderful."[39]

A blanket of five hundred roses was laid across the shoulders of Dancer's Image. Peter Fuller and Lou Cavalaris stood at the colt's head; a smiling Bobby Ussery flashed a victory sign.

Fuller, his wife, Joan, and five of their seven children crowded onto the elevated winner's stand in the infield a few minutes later. Cavalaris was there,

Jockey Bobby Ussery flashed a victory sign in the winner's circle. A smiling Peter Fuller and his family are at the horse's head. *George Featherston photo. Courtesy of the* Thoroughbred Times.

SEVENTH RACE
CD 34634
May 4. 1968

1 1-4 MILES. (Northern Dancer. May 2. 1964. 2:00. 3. 126.) Ninety-fourth running KENTUCKY DERBY. Scale weights. $125,000 added. 3-year-olds. By subscription of $100 each in cash which covers nomination for both the Kentucky Derby and Derby Trial. All nomination fees to Derby winner, $500 to pass the entry box, $1,000 additional to start, $125,000 added, of which $25,000 to second, $12,500 to third, $5,000 to fourth. $100,000 guaranteed to winner (to be divided equally in event of a dead heat). Weight, 126 lbs. The owner of the winner to receive a gold trophy. A nomnation may be withdrawn before time of closing nominations. Closed Thursday, Feb. 15, 1968, with 191 nominations.
Value of race $165,100. Value to winner $122,600; second, $25,000; third, $12,500; fourth, $5,000.
Mutuel Pool, $2,350,470.

Inc▶	Horses	Eq't	A	Wt	PP	¼	½	¾	1	Str	Fin	Jockeys	Owners	Odds to $1
34451Aqu1	—Dancer's Image		3	126	12	14	14	10½	8^{h}	1^{1}	$1^{1\frac{1}{2}}$	R Ussery	Peter Fuller	3.60
34402Kee1	—Forward Pass	b	3	126	13	3^{2}	4^{4}	3^{4}	2^{2}	2½	2^{nk}	I Valenz'ela	Calumet Farm	2.20
34402Kee3	—Francie's Hat		3	126	10	11^{3}	11^{2}	7^{2}	7^{2}	4^{2}	$3^{2\frac{1}{2}}$	E Fires	Saddle Rock Farm	23.50
34402Kee2	—T. V. C'mercial	b	3	126	2	9½	8^{1}	9^{1}	6½	5^{h}	4^{1}	H Grant	Bwamazon Farm	24.00
34307CD4	—Kentucky Sherry		3	126	4	1½	1^{2}	1^{2}	1^{h}	3^{2}	5^{1}	J Combest	Mrs Joe W Brown	f-14.70
34325CD2	—Jig Time	b	3	126	3	$7^{1\frac{1}{2}}$	6½	6½	4^{h}	6^{h}	6½	R Brouss'rd	Cragwood Stable	36.30
34425GG2	—Don B.		3	126	7	5^{2}	5^{2}	5^{1}	$5^{1\frac{1}{2}}$	7^{4}	7^{5}	D Pierce	D B Wood	35.50
34307CD2	—Trouble Brewing		3	126	5	12½	9^{1}	11^{2}	13^{4}	12^{4}	8^{nk}	B Thornb'rg	Coventry Rock Farm	f-14.70
34325CD1	—Proper Proof		3	126	11	13^{3}	12^{1}	12^{2}	11^{2}	$8^{1\frac{1}{2}}$	9^{4}	J Sellers	Mrs Montgomery Fisher	9.90
34325CD4	—Te Vega	b	3	126	6	8^{h}	13^{h}	13^{1}	12^{2}	9^{2}	10¾	M Mang'llo	F C Sullivan	f-14.70
34307CD1	—Captain's Gig		3	126	9	2^{h}	2^{h}	2^{1}	3^{2}	10^{2}	$11^{1\frac{1}{2}}$	M Ycaza	Cain Hoy Stable	6.10
34451Aqu2	—Iron Ruler		3	126	1	10½	7½	8½	9^{h}	11^{1}	12^{3}	B Baeza	October House Farm	5.70
34325CD3	—Verbatim	b	3	126	8	6^{h}	10^{h}	14	14	14	13no	A Cord'o Jr	Elmendorf	37.40
34402Kee5	—Gl'ming Sword	b	3	126	14	4½	3½	4^{h}	10^{2}	13^{1}	14	E Belmonte	C V Whitney	31.20

f-Mutuel field.

Time, :22⅕, :45⅘, 1:09⅘, 1:36⅕, 2:02⅕. Track fast.

$2 Mutuel Prices:

9-DANCER'S IMAGE	9.20	4.40	4.00
10-FORWARD PASS		4.20	3.20
7-FRANCIE'S HAT			6.40

Gr. c, by Native Dancer—Noors Image, by Noor. Trainer, L. C. Cavalaris, Jr. Bred by P. Fuller (Md.).
IN GATE—4:40. OFF AT 4:40½ EASTERN DAYLIGHT TIME. Start good. Won driving.

DANCER'S IMAGE, void of speed through the early stages after being bumped at the start, commenced a rally after three-quarters to advance between horses on the second turn, cut back to the inside when clear entering the stretch at which point his rider dropped his whip. Responding to a vigorous hand ride the colt continued to save ground to take command nearing the furlong marker and was hard pressed to edge FORWARD PASS. The latter broke alertly only to be bumped and knocked into the winner, continued gamely while maintaining a forward position along the outside, moved boldly to take command between calls in the upper stretch and held on stubbornly in a prolonged drive. FRANCIE'S HAT, allowed to settle in stride, commenced a rally after three-quarters and finished full of run. T. V. COMMERCIAL closed some ground in his late rally but could not seriously menace. KENTUCKY SHERRY broke in stride to make the pace under good rating, saved ground to the stretch where he drifted out while tiring. JIG TIME faltered after making a menacing bid on the second turn. PROPER PROOF was always outrun. CAPTAIN'S GIG tired badly after prompting the issue for three-quarters. IRON RULER failed to enter contention. GLEAMING SWORD broke alertly but sharply to the inside to bump with FORWARD PASS, continued in a forward position for five furlongs and commenced dropping back steadily.

The official Kentucky Derby chart was published before the Dancer's Image controversy was made public. *Copyrighted c. 2011 by Daily Racing Form, LLC, and Equibase Company. Reprinted with permission of the copyright owner.*

as was Ussery. Governor Louie B. Nunn presented the $5,000 gold winner's trophy to Fuller and smaller replicas to the trainer and jockey.

Fuller was standing where every Thoroughbred owner longed to be, holding the trophy for winning the most important horse race in the world.

It was "the most wonderful week of my life," he said.[40]

Chapter 6

WELCOME TO OZ

It's called the "spit box" for a reason.

When testing for prohibited medications began, a sample of a horse's saliva was collected for the analysis. As laboratory procedures became more sophisticated, urine replaced saliva as the medium of choice for testing, but the original nickname stuck. Considering the possibilities, some of them unprintable, that is probably a good thing. A trip to the spit box by the winner of a race nearly always was just a formality required by the rules, and no one expected testing for the 1968 Kentucky Derby to be any different.

After the television cameras shut down, the winner's circle celebration and general hoopla that accompany a Derby victory moved en masse from the infield to the track's private dining room for the traditional postrace party. Churchill Downs president Wathen Knebelkamp hosted the annual affair, and teetotaler Peter Fuller was the life of the party. The victory was the fulfillment of every Thoroughbred owner's dream, and Fuller was determined to enjoy every second of the experience.

Robert Barnard was going to miss the festivities. He did not care for champagne anyway, and he had another job to do. Barnard had to accompany Dancer's Image to the spit box, a detention area set aside at Barn 17 where samples of the horse's saliva and urine would be collected for drug testing.

"Sure it's a thrill to see your horse come across the wire," the assistant trainer said as he walked beside Dancer's Image, "but after he crosses it, it's back to the same routine."[41] The "same routine" at the spit box was dictated by rules handed down by the Kentucky State Racing Commission. Samples

The winner heads to the winner's circle, while the other horses return to the barns. *Winants Brothers photo. Courtesy of the* Blood-Horse.

were collected for drug testing from the winners of every race on every card, and the commissioners had the discretion to select other horses as well. Despite that discretion and the race's obvious importance to everyone involved, saliva and urine were obtained from two—and only two—horses in the Derby field. Those horses were Dancer's Image and Kentucky Sherry, the pacesetter that almost stole the race before eventually tiring and finishing fifth. None of the other horses, including the beaten favorite Forward Pass, were tested.

As soon as Dancer's Image arrived at the detention barn, eight ounces of sterile water were squirted into the horse's mouth. The water that dribbled out was caught in a stainless steel pan and sealed in a clean bottle for later chemical analysis.[42] Collecting a urine sample from Dancer's Image was a little more complicated than having the horse slobber in a pan. Horses generally urinate when they need to, not when it might be convenient for the people standing around watching.

Dancer's Image was walked under the shed row for a half hour to finish cooling out, and then the serious waiting began. Assistant Veterinarian George Dickinson had the first watch, standing at the ready with an eight-ounce bottle to collect the horse's urine, but Dancer's Image did not deliver. Sidney Turner, another official testing veterinarian, took over after thirty minutes, and a urine sample finally was collected around 7:00 p.m. By the time the collection process was finished, Dancer's Image had been in the detention barn for a little under two hours. Barnard was a constant observer.

"He watched me the whole time I was with the horse," Dr. Turner said.[43]

The bottles containing the samples collected from Dancer's Image were sealed, and small cardboard tags were attached—white with the number 3956S for saliva, and yellow, appropriately, for urine with the number 3956U. Each card had two parts, one that stayed with the saliva or urine sample and was identified only by a number, and a second, detachable part that included the number and the name of the horse that provided the sample. The parts of the cards matching the specific sample numbers to Dancer's Image were detached by the supervising veterinarian and sealed in an envelope with cards identifying samples from winners of the day's other races. The envelope was delivered to the stewards' office, where the tags were locked up for safekeeping.

James W. Chinn was the next individual to handle the saliva and urine samples collected on Derby Day. The racing commission contracted out drug testing at the state's tracks to Kenneth Smith's Louisville Testing Laboratory, Inc., and Smith used a trailer outfitted with some fairly sophisticated laboratory equipment as a mobile testing facility. The blue and white mobile lab was parked in a fenced-off area of the backstretch near the spit box. Chinn, whose qualifications included "some college" and several years of on-the-job training, was the laboratory technician on duty. When he received the samples and started his preliminary tests that evening, he had no idea which sample came from which horse, a level of anonymity essential to the integrity of the entire drug testing process.

To speed things along, Chinn mixed a portion of sample 3956U with urine collected from two other unidentified horses and set about conducting a preliminary screening test on the composite sample. A negative result for the composite would mean that all three samples showed no traces of prohibited medications. That was the expected outcome; no winner had come up positive for phenylbutazone in Kentucky since testing started in 1962. A positive result, on the other hand, would indicate that at least one of the urine samples that went into the mix contained a prohibited medication. The Vitali test, for that was what the screening test was called, was not specific for a particular drug, and further chemical analysis would be required to narrow down the list of possible medications.

Chinn added a solvent to the composite to extract drug residue, if there was any in the sample. After a bit of the extract had been allowed to dry on a small white plate, Chinn added a drop of fuming nitric acid to what was left. After that mixture had dried out, a drop of alcoholic potassium hydroxide was added. No change in color indicated a negative result. That was what Chinn expected, and that was the result he got from the other composite samples he tested that evening.

Unexpectedly, however, extract from the composite containing urine from sample 3956U changed color. This was sufficient for Chinn to suspect a prohibited medication and to call the test result "positive," although positive for what he could not say. The Vitali test was nonspecific, so Chinn did not know for certain which drug—although he suspected phenylbutazone—or which horse. All Chinn could say with any degree of certainty was that at least one of three so far unidentified horses that raced on Derby Day had what appeared to be a positive test for something.

It was around 7:30 p.m., and the winner's party still was in full swing. The Fuller entourage was celebrating, and Churchill Downs president Wathen Knebelkamp finally was starting to relax.

"Man, I'm telling you," Knebelkamp said at one point, "when the 'official' sign goes up, I'm one happy fellah."[44]

***

There was a protocol to be followed in the unlikely event of a positive test.[45]

Jimmy Chinn telephoned laboratory supervisor Maurice Cusick, who managed to track down Kenneth W. Smith, Kentucky's designated "racing chemist." Smith cut short his dinner at Audubon Country Club, and by 9:00 p.m., Smith, Cusick and Chinn met at the Chestnut Street office of Louisville Testing Laboratory. Chinn had with him the composite sample, the three individual urine samples that contributed to the composite and the white "spotplate" that he used as a reference to note the color change and to call the composite Vitali test "positive."

The first order of business was determining which of the three numbered urine samples actually was positive for something that should not have been there. Separate Vitali color tests performed on the three individual samples indicated that number 3956U (designated Lab Sample 9) was the culprit. The two other individual samples were discarded. To Smith, the color change of the extract on the white spotplate suggested the presence of phenylbutazone or a metabolite of the drug. He made a black and white Polaroid photograph to document the result.

This was a curious choice if Smith intended to make a record of the test to support his conclusion. Accurate interpretation of a Vitali result depends on changes in color, and the nuances of color obviously cannot be seen in a black and white image. Smith's photograph might show that there was a color change of some kind, but it was useless as either supporting or refuting his conclusion about the presence of phenylbutazone.

A Vitali test does not produce an objective "yes" or "no" result that clearly indicates the presence of Bute in a urine sample. If phenylbutazone is present, the extract when tested will show a color ranging from reddish-purple to brown to almost black. The more Bute in the sample, the closer to black the color will be. What complicates things is that other drugs exhibit similar color changes when subjected to a Vitali test. The color change must be interpreted by someone with experience in reading Vitali results. It is a completely subjective judgment, an expert conclusion that is only as good as the "expert" looking at the spotplate. Since 1962, when Kentucky began testing for phenylbutazone, Smith never had found a positive for the drug in a racehorse.

Sample 3956U also was subjected to microcrystal analysis, a test that is old, simple and relatively specific. A sample suspected of containing a drug is mixed with a reagent, and the crystals that form from the chemical reaction are examined under a microscope.[46] Like a Vitali result, though, accurate interpretation of microcrystals to identify a specific drug depends on the expertise of the individual looking through the microscope. Smith made some Polaroid photographs of the crystals and called these tests positive for phenylbutazone as well.

At some point late on Saturday evening, Smith called state steward Lewis O. Finley to report a problem with a sample from one of the races on Derby Day. Finley, along with Leo O'Donnell and John G. Goode, were the three stewards employed by the racing commission and the track to ensure compliance with the rules of racing. Although Smith felt that the Vitali and microcrystal tests were positive for phenylbutazone, he was not definite about his findings in the initial call to Finley, calling the sample "suspicious."[47]

Smith asked Finley what to do. Sunday was a dark day at Churchill Downs, and on an ordinary weekend, the chemist's report for a Saturday card, even one including a positive drug test, would not be submitted to the stewards until the following Monday. This was not an ordinary weekend, of course, and Smith's question was a good one. Despite the significance of a potential drug positive on Derby Day, Finley elected to follow the usual procedure.

"Submit your report Monday morning," the commission steward told Smith, "the same as always. Good night."[48]

***

The chemist rolled out the big gun around midnight—or at least he tried to.

Ultraviolet spectrophotometry was the gold standard for drug analysis in 1968, and Smith usually had two different machines at his disposal. The Beckman Model DU spectrophotometer at the Chestnut Street Laboratory did not work, however, so Smith, Cusick and Chinn drove back out to the mobile laboratory at Churchill Downs to use a different machine, a newer Beckman Model DK-2. The DK-2 machine had been calibrated and tested a few days earlier by a technician from the manufacturer, and at that time, it was found to be in proper working order.

When light of a specific wavelength (called monochromatic light) is passed through a sample of urine containing an unknown or suspected drug, some of the light is transmitted and some is absorbed by the drug. Just how much light is absorbed is directly related to the wavelength of the light. A spectrophotometer passes light at varying wavelengths through a sample and displays the percentage of absorption at each wavelength.

When the absorption percentages are plotted on a piece of graph paper (by the machine with the DK-2, by hand with the Model DU) a familiar bell-shaped curve is produced. The more different wavelengths tested, the more accurate the resulting curve. The complete figure is called the sample's "absorption spectrum." The topmost point on the graph will indicate the single wavelength at which the unknown compound absorbed the most light.

The point of maximum absorption is characteristic of a specific compound and can be a useful tool for identification of a suspected drug. The absorption maximum for pure phenylbutazone is 265 nanometers; for phenylbutazone in horse urine, the absorption maximum is lower and may range from 260 to 265 nanometers. Contaminants in the urine sample may skew the results even further by altering the absorption maximum for Bute and by producing other peaks, called "shoulders," that are unrelated to presence of the suspected drug.

Smith prepared the samples, calibrated the DK-2 machine and ran the tests while Cusick and Chinn stood by and watched. The chemist generated two separate absorption spectra for sample 3956U, the first in solution with a basic buffer and the second in solution with an acidic buffer. Solutions of the basic and acidic buffers without any of Sample 3956U added were used as references. Smith thought the base curve "compared favorably" with an absorption spectrum for phenylbutazone he found in a book. Apparently satisfied with the resulting graphs, both of which were plotted on the same sheet of graph paper, Smith did not repeat the tests. He labeled the graphs with the sample number and the date—May 5, 1968, since it was after midnight—and initialed the paper. Cusick and Chinn added their initials to the graphs and then everyone went home for the night.

There must have been some lingering doubts in Smith's mind, though, because he was back at work on Sunday at the Chestnut Street lab. He worked alone in the lab from 9:30 a.m. until 12:30 p.m., left for a few hours and then returned and stayed from 6:30 p.m. until around 10:00 p.m. He repeated the microcrystal tests and made a second set of photographs. He did not label either set of microcrystal images with the day they were taken, an oversight typical of a general lack of documentation for all the tests done on Sample 3956U.

Smith also ran a Mandelin test, an analysis similar to the earlier Vitali test but using a different reagent to elicit a color change in the sample. As with the Vitali test, the Mandelin test was nonspecific for phenylbutazone, and a correct interpretation of the color change was subjective and based on the chemist's experience. Smith made no photographs of those test results. Nor did he return to the mobile laboratory to run another set of samples through the only working spectrophotometer he had at his disposal. There apparently was no need. Smith already thought the Saturday evening and Sunday test results were positive for phenylbutazone. He was prepared to "stake his career" on the result.[49]

Then two curious things happened.

Smith did not telephone Finley to update the commission steward on the new round of test results. Perhaps he was relying on Finley's earlier admonition to follow standard reporting procedure and wait until Monday. Or perhaps Smith still had doubts about the test results. Before he left the lab on Sunday evening, Smith poured a small portion of Sample 3956U into a bottle, sealed it and mailed the sample to Lewis E. Harris, a colleague who ran the drug testing laboratory for the Nebraska Racing Commission. He dropped the sample in the mail and then telephoned Harris to tell him the sample was coming. He wondered whether Harris "could detect phenylbutazone" in the sample.

***

Smith finally telephoned Lewis Finley at his Georgetown, Kentucky home early on Monday morning to report the positive test and to relay the sample number—3956U. Later that morning at Churchill Downs, Finley and the other stewards opened the sealed envelope of sample cards and matched Sample 3956U with the name of the Derby winner, Dancer's Image. Based only on Smith's telephone call, because the chemist had not yet delivered his written report of the positive drug test, the stewards immediately passed the bombshell news along to Wathen Knebelkamp, president of Churchill Downs, and to George E. Egger, chairman of the Kentucky State Racing Commission.

When Smith showed up at the stewards' office later in the day, he still did not have written confirmation of the positive test results. Instead, he turned in negative reports for tests on the other winners on Derby Day and presented a brief report stating that "further testing was necessary" for Sample 3956U. He requested additional time to report his findings.[50] Finley was "surprised" and "dumbfounded" by this turn of events.[51]

Smith explained that he had sent a sample to an out-of-state chemist for confirmation of the positive test results he had obtained over the weekend. The stewards, however, did not appear to be even remotely interested in any further delay.

Finley told Smith that the stewards were not interested in the results of anyone else's tests. Smith was the official chemist for the racing commission, Finley said, and Smith's test results were the only ones that mattered.[52] Donnell and Goode concurred.

Smith returned to the mobile laboratory, completed his written report on the positive test results for Sample 3956U and delivered the requested positive report to the stewards.[53]

Smith had not heard anything from Harris, the chemist in Nebraska, and after a couple of telephone calls, he learned that the sample had not arrived. Neither Smith nor the stewards mentioned to anyone else that another chemist at an out-of-state lab had been asked to test the urine collected from Dancer's Image.

Lou Cavalaris was at home in Toronto when he heard the news. Someone from Churchill Downs called the trainer and told him that Dancer's Image had tested positive for Bute. He asked Cavalaris to return to Louisville as soon as possible.

"The words staggered me," said Cavalaris, who had a squeaky-clean record and a reputation for honesty everywhere he raced. "I was spellbound. I just stood there. I've been in this game 21 years and I've never done anything wrong yet. I'm innocent and so are my men. They love Dancer's Image, just as I do."[54]

With Cavalaris unavailable, Alvin Schwem, head of security for Churchill Downs, and George Korjenek from the Thoroughbred Racing Protective Bureau interviewed assistant trainer Robert Barnard and groom Russell Parchen. The investigators also searched the barn and the tack room where Barnard and Parchen slept. They also examined the grain in the feed room, all without finding anything to suggest how Dancer's Image might have been medicated with Bute. Or, for that matter, whether the horse even had the drug in his system on race day.

Peter Fuller still was in Louisville when word reached him. He made another call to his friend Warner Jones, said "I'm not taking this crap" and asked Jones to recommend a good lawyer. Jones came up with the name of Arthur Grafton, a prominent local attorney and Thoroughbred owner.[55]

Edward S. Bonnie, a young lawyer and horseman, came on board at the suggestion of Dr. Harthill. Stuart E. Lampe, from the same firm as Grafton, filled out Fuller's legal team.

***

Cavalaris returned to Louisville on Monday evening. He met with the stewards the next morning for "official" notification of the test results, still thoroughly baffled about the whole mess.

Knebelkamp broke the news about Dancer's Image a few hours later during an early afternoon press conference at Churchill Downs, when he read a brief statement from the stewards.[56] It was the first public announcement of Smith's test results, and Knebelkamp managed only to further muddy the waters with his comments.

He first misspoke about the nature of the stewards' preliminary announcement of the positive drug test, calling it an "official ruling" when it was not. The stewards had inadvertently issued their statement on a piece of paper with the heading "Steward's Ruling," but the stewards could only announce a "ruling" that carried any weight after a hearing. That hearing would not take place for a week, and any official ruling would have to wait.

Knebelkamp then said that Dancer's Image would be disqualified and Forward Pass made the winner of the Derby. He opined that if Forward Pass managed to win the Preakness Stakes and Belmont Stakes, the horse would be a Triple Crown winner. Kentucky rules were not as expansive as Knebelkamp made them out to be, however. A drug positive would result in a redistribution of the purse, but the rules were specific that the order of finish would not change. The winner's share of the purse might go to Forward Pass, but Dancer's Image could not be disqualified under the rules.

"Winning the Kentucky Derby was the most fantastic thrill I've ever had," Fuller told reporters. "And this experience today is by far the biggest disappointment."[57]

Amazingly, things would get even worse.

***

Certainly from the moment Kenneth Smith handed in his written report on Monday and probably from his first telephone call to Lewis Finley two days earlier, the question of whether Dancer's Image actually raced with Bute in his system in the Derby was almost a nonissue for the stewards. Smith was the official racing chemist, he called a "positive" on the horse, enough said. The stewards were "going on the findings of Kenneth Smith."[58]

(Although Smith told the stewards that he would stake his career and his life on the initial positive test results,[59] he repeated his tests on Tuesday. Smith eventually reported similar results, but those subsequent tests were conducted after the public announcement identifying Dancer's Image as the horse that tested positive for Bute. The later tests were subject to many of the same criticisms as Smith's initial tests and, because of their timing, could not have contributed to the stewards' announcement that Dancer's Image had tested positive.)

A request to see hard data and documentation for Smith's testing procedures was granted, reluctantly and only in part, the morning the hearing started. A request for urine testing by an independent laboratory was denied because the sample supposedly had been used up in Smith's analysis. The sample Smith dispatched to Lewis Harris in Nebraska was not disclosed at the hearing, and the results of that independent analysis would not be revealed for almost half a year. As far as Fuller and his attorneys knew at the time, only Smith, Cusick and Chinn had actually tested Sample 3956U.

Grafton and Bonnie challenged Smith's findings throughout the three-day hearing. They raised questions and objections about every aspect of the collection and testing procedures, but the attorneys were trying to upend a foregone conclusion. The stewards had one objective during the hearing, and it was not to question Smith's findings or his competence to make them. Instead, the stewards wanted to find someone to blame.

At that, they failed.

The closed hearing seemed to last forever, especially for the reporters who milled around outside the hearing room waiting for something—anything—to happen that might break the monotony. The *Daily Racing Form* even reported on the meals that were carried in during each session: "cold cuts, potato salads, finger sandwiches, old fashioned pound cake, and coffee" for lunch the first day.[60]

On Monday, the hearing ran until 8:15 p.m.; the second day did not break up until after 2:00 a.m. the following morning; the final day concluded around 5:30 p.m. Over the course of three mind-numbing days, a total of eleven witnesses testified, and some 1,200 pages of sworn testimony were generated. It took more than six hours to fine-tune the language of the ruling, but in the end, there were no surprises. The stewards made only one finding of fact, that Dancer's Image had won the Kentucky Derby with phenylbutazone in his system, and that was a conclusion the stewards went into the hearing room already inclined to reach.[61]

The ruling redistributed the Derby purse, awarding $122,600 to Forward Pass, $25,000 to Francie's Hat, $12,500 to T.V. Commercial and $5,000 to Kentucky Sherry (the only other horse in the field whose urine and saliva had been tested for drugs).

Cavalaris and Barnard each was suspended for thirty days but not because there was even the slightest evidence that either one of them did anything wrong. Rules in Kentucky and in every other state with horse racing turn the usual guarantee of "innocent until proven guilty" on its head. A trainer typically is responsible for the condition of horses in his care, even without a showing of any fault on the trainer's part, and Cavalaris and Barnard were punished on that basis alone.

Cavalaris and Barnard appealed the suspensions and asked for a stay of their punishments until the appeal was resolved. The racing commission denied the request for a stay and scheduled a hearing on the suspensions for early June. A hearing would be meaningless at that point, though, because the thirty-day suspensions would expire a few days later. Cavalaris and Barnard dismissed their appeals and served their thirty-day suspensions.

The suspension of Cavalaris was especially troubling because Dancer's Image was scheduled to run in the Preakness Stakes in a few days. Peter Fuller initially announced that the horse would not run in the Preakness if Cavalaris could not train him, but the owner eventually relented. Fuller's farm manager, Bob Casey, substituted for Cavalaris at Pimlico Race Course.

Having decided that Dancer's Image had, in fact, received an illegal dose of Bute prior to the Derby, the stewards ultimately were at a loss about how it happened, when it happened or who was responsible. The question that intrigued everyone was not answered, although the stewards did raise a cloud of suspicion by mentioning some "other matters" that deserved further investigation. What those "matters" were would not become public for several months.

Although the stewards' hearing shed almost no new light on what actually happened with Dancer's Image prior to the Derby, the lengthy proceeding did reaffirm the peculiar status enjoyed by racing chemists. Like the *Wizard of Oz*, chemists labored in their secret laboratories, doing things with chemicals and mysterious machines that hardly anyone understood. When they came out to announce a "positive" for a horse, the strength of their proclamation was enough. Nothing else needed to be said. No further proof was required by the stewards.

The next step for Peter Fuller was an appeal of the stewards' ruling to the Kentucky State Racing Commission. If Fuller was going to win that appeal, he and his attorneys would have to topple the screen of secrecy surrounding the racing chemist's lab and show that there was no magic involved and, for Dancer's Image at least, not much good science, either.

Chapter 7

AN UNBELIEVABLE
WITNESS

On Monday after the Kentucky Derby, late in the evening, people started drifting into Peter Fuller's room at the Brown Suburban Motel on Bardstown Road. The Fuller entourage had set up shop in the motel almost a week earlier, but the tone of this meeting was far different from the euphoria that followed the Kentucky Derby.

The positive drug test for Dancer's Image would not be public knowledge for another twelve hours, not until Wathen Knebelkamp's press conference the next day, but everyone associated with the horse already knew about it. Fuller and Cavalaris had gotten unofficial notification, and anyone on the backstretch who saw investigators shaking down the Harthill Barn knew that something was amiss.

Fuller was there, as were trainer Lou Cavalaris, who had rushed back to Louisville from his home in Toronto; Dr. Alex Harthill; Fuller's farm manager, Bob Casey; Paul Hyatt; the insurance agent, Ed McGrath; and Warner Jones. They were joined by Arthur Grafton, the attorney recommended to Fuller by Jones, Stuart Lampe and Ned Bonnie.

In other circumstances, this might have been a meeting for damage control, to figure out how to make the best of an unbelievably bad situation. But Peter Fuller had faith in his horse and in his trainer. He was a fighter, and he was totally unwilling to accept the disastrous turn of events.

With little preamble, Fuller started around the room asking if anyone had a theory to win the case against Dancer's Image. No one did, not until Fuller's

Peter Fuller. *George
Featherston photo.
Courtesy of the*
Thoroughbred
Times.

attention settled on Bonnie. He was the youngest man in the room, and the least experienced, and everyone did a double take when he spoke up: "Yes, I do."

Bonnie was starting to make a name for himself in equine medication cases, and he had some prior experience dealing with Kenneth Smith, the chemist who called the "positive" on Fuller's horse. The only way to win, Bonnie said, was to attack the efficacy of the entire postrace testing procedure, question it from start to finish, demand proof not opinion. He had little respect for Smith's competence in the laboratory, and he thought the state's official chemist was the weak link.

Bonnie first came up against Smith a few years earlier, when he represented an owner and trainer whose horse had tested positive for a prohibited drug. That case involved an inexpensive horse and a small purse, and neither the owner nor the trainer could afford to fight the ruling. Peter Fuller, though, had the resources and the resolve to mount a serious challenge to Smith's tests.[62]

No one had ever challenged a racing commission chemist before, at least not in the way Bonnie suggested. If it could be proved that Smith's conclusion about the urine sample containing Bute was wrong, Fuller would win and Dancer's Image would be vindicated, but that would be a difficult case to make. It might be impossible without independent testing, and no one knew whether that was even a possibility. The rules did not require retention of a portion of the urine for confirmatory testing. If Sample 3956U was gone, Fuller had no recourse.

Proving that Smith was incompetent, on the other hand, and that his testing procedures were so flawed that none of his results could be trusted, might be achievable—at least Bonnie thought so. For this strategy to work,

Fuller and his attorneys would need the data and documentation for Smith's tests and the assistance of experts to help make sense of it all. The planned attack was not perfect. Proving that Kenneth Smith was incompetent in general did not necessarily mean that a particular result was wrong.

Fuller went around the motel room again, asking if anyone had a better theory. No one did. A hasty division of labor put Grafton in charge of assembling the factual elements of the case and left the technical aspects of the challenge to Smith's competence in Bonnie's hands.

The strategy was unsuccessful in the stewards' hearing. There had been very little time to prepare, Smith had been far less than forthcoming with his hard data and records, nothing remained of Sample 3956U for independent tests and the reluctance of one racing chemist to testify against another was beginning to be apparent. Add in the stewards' proclivity to accept Smith's conclusions at face value, and the ruling against Dancer's Image probably was inevitable.

Peter Fuller's legal team: Edward S. Bonnie, Arthur Grafton and Stuart Lampe. *Courtesy of the* Blood-Horse.

Round one was finished—advantage to the stewards—but the fight was far from over.

Round two—a hearing in front of the Kentucky State Racing Commission—would be a tough one. While it might not be fair to claim that the commissioners did nothing except rubber stamp the stewards' rulings, it was a fact that no stewards' ruling ever had been overturned by a racing commission in the state.[63]

***

Louie B. Nunn won a hard-fought election in 1967 to become Kentucky's first Republican governor in twenty-four years. When Nunn took office in December, he made wholesale changes at every level of state government. That was to be expected; the spoils system always had been alive and well in Kentucky. What came as a minor surprise was his selection for chairman of the Kentucky State Racing Commission. George E. Egger was a successful businessman and a loyal political supporter who headed Nunn's campaign finance committee, but he was not a horseman—never had been. Egger's primary qualifications for the job, apart from his political leanings, seemed to be that several of his friends raced Thoroughbreds.

Nunn's other appointees—Laban Jackson, John A. Bell III, Stanley Lambert and J.S. Friedberg—all were prominent owners and breeders, though, and the new commission quickly gained a reputation among many horsemen for being progressive and genuinely concerned about racing. The Dancer's Image case would be the first serious test for Egger and company and would make obvious an inherent conflict between the administrative and judicial functions of the racing commission.

Most of the time, the racing commission did what governmental agencies usually do; the commissioners were administrators, and they administrated. They parceled out racing dates among the state's tracks, wrote and revised the Rules of Racing, hired employees, issued licenses to owners and trainers and had general oversight of horse racing in Kentucky. More importantly, the commission also was charged with "maintaining integrity and honesty in racing," which involved enforcement of the commission's own rules.

As part of its enforcement function, the racing commission served as the reviewing body for all rulings made by the stewards. The commission was not an appellate court, and the commissioners were not judges in any official sense, but they necessarily took on that role when a stewards' ruling

The Kentucky State Racing Commission: J.S. Friedberg, John A. Bell III, George E. Egger, Laban Jackson and Stanley Lambert. *Courtesy of the* Blood-Horse.

was appealed. It was this quasijudicial function that led to an unavoidable conflict of interest. Even if the commissioners all were men of integrity and there was no reason to think that they were not, impartiality must be strained when men are asked to adjudicate questions about rules of their own making and about the competence and reliability of employees they hired.

The first stumbling block for Fuller was his attorneys' request for full discovery prior to the commission hearing. The parties involved in civil litigation are allowed to obtain information from the other side to help prepare their cases and to avoid surprise at trial, and Fuller's attorneys made a similar prehearing request. It was denied. Fuller asked the Franklin Circuit Court for help and eventually got a ruling granting the discovery request. The commission appealed, and Kentucky's highest court affirmed the lower court's order.

The procedural sideshow took months from start to finish and pushed the commission hearing from June until November. For Fuller, the delay was productive for a couple of reasons. The hearing originally had been scheduled for June 12, a mere nine days after the appeal was filed. The unplanned delay gave the attorneys several months instead of a few days to review some 1,200 pages of testimony from the stewards' hearing. Also, his legal team eventually received most of the documentary evidence they wanted, and depositions of Smith, Cusick and Chinn, along with the experts who would testify for the commission, were scheduled. Assistant Attorney General George F. Rabe, lead counsel representing the racing commission, deposed Cavalaris, Barnard and Fuller's experts.

During Smith's deposition in October, Fuller's attorneys learned for the first time that the chemist had sent a sample to Lewis Harris in Nebraska on the Sunday after the Derby, and that Sample 3956U had been subjected to additional tests by Smith on Tuesday after the positive result for Dancer's Image had been made public. Both events could be interpreted as signs of doubt about the result on Smith's part; information about the events was not disclosed to Fuller and his attorneys for months.

Cavalaris and Barnard had nothing to add regarding Smith's testing procedures. However, they could talk about the physical condition of Dancer's Image, both before and after the Derby, and Rabe seemed interested in trying to establish that the horse was a cripple that could not win the Derby without prohibited medication. Even if true, which Fuller's attorneys argued was not the case, the horse's condition was hardly relevant to the reliability of Smith's chemical tests.

The commission hearing finally got underway on November 18, 1968, and ran through December 7. The venue was moved from the relatively intimate setting for the stewards' hearing at Churchill Downs to the state fairgrounds in Louisville. The Kentucky Fair and Exposition Center was home to a world's championship horse show, livestock exhibitions, college and high school basketball games, ice shows, professional wrestling and, appropriately, the circus.

Before any testimony was taken, Fuller's attorneys asked to conduct *voir dire* examinations of the five commissioners. The purpose, they said, was to ferret out any prejudices the commissioners might have that would affect their adjudication of Fuller's appeal. Did the commissioners, for example, harbor any animosity toward Fuller after being sued and losing on the discovery question?

If the commissioners started with the assumption that Kenneth Smith was correct in his conclusions, as Fuller's team maintained the stewards had done at the earlier hearing, they should be unqualified to decide the appeal. *Voir dire* for potential jurors—but not for judges—is common in civil and criminal trials. Because the commissioners would serve dual duty as judges and as jurors in the hearing, the attorneys reasoned that voir dire was appropriate.

Like the original discovery request, the *voir dire* request was denied. (Months later, depositions of the five commissioners were taken by permission of the

An Unbelievable Witness

Franklin Circuit Court. The commissioners' testimony suggested that they had gone into the hearing with the infallibility of Kenneth Smith and his findings uppermost in their minds.)

***

Peter Fuller was the first witness to testify, and he made an impassioned statement in support of his horse and his trainer.

> *I am making this appeal because I know that I didn't do anything wrong. I believe the members of my organization didn't do anything wrong, and I feel that I should know, should find out, what did go wrong.*
>
> *I think I have to speak personally, and I will try to keep any sentiment out of this thing, and yet at the same time it enters into it. Because you have to realize that when you are in the position that I was in...and am fortunate enough to have a horse in the Derby...it just doesn't happen every day. It means an awful lot.*
>
> *And when you have raised the horse yourself, and you have bred him and you have watched him grow and you have admittedly made mistakes with him, and you have good things with him and you have all the experience with the horse, then it's a very real thing. And to hear my horse described as some kind of cripple, to hear him described, or to feel...that this horse is owned by some guy that had a lot of people down to the Derby and he's going to run, that just isn't the way it is.*
>
> *I do not feel in any way that I am a poor sport. As a matter of fact, I have indulged in athletics and sports all my life. And one thing that I have learned to do is to lose gracefully. And I have had a lot of chance to study it, because I have lost quite a bit, and I have had a lot of practice at it. So I know what it is to lose.*
>
> *I don't believe I am a cry-baby, and I am extremely fond of racing, I've been in racing for 15 years. I don't want to do anything in the world to hurt racing anywhere, and certainly not in Kentucky.*
>
> *However, something went wrong, and I felt that I should find out what was wrong...This horse is no phony horse, this horse didn't win races with mirrors. This horse won races on his ability, not with the help of anything except the ability he had.*
>
> *I have to clear my horse's name.*[64]

Fuller's testimony may have been the only understandable words uttered by anyone in the hearing room for days. The proceeding quickly turned into a battle of experts, with chemist Kenneth Smith standing precariously in no man's land. Not one of the commissioners went into the hearing with a formal grounding in chemistry, but after weeks of testimony that often was technical, arcane and probably interminably boring, they must have felt like candidates for graduate degrees in the subject.

Fuller seemed to have the edge during the first week and a half.

Smith spent thirteen hours on the witness stand during three days, treated as a hostile witness by Fuller's attorneys, and his testimony was riddled with contradictions and lapses of memory. Kent Hollingsworth, whose coverage for the *Blood-Horse* magazine was the most comprehensive reporting on the event, commented: "Smith set a track record for 'I can't recalls,' and at one point responded, 'As I recall…I don't recall.'"[65] Smith did reaffirm his opinion that the series of tests he performed proved the presence of phenylbutazone.

After another lapse of memory, the following exchange took place:

> *Kenneth Smith: "I apologize, Mr. Grafton, I don't recall."*
> *Assistant Attorney General George Rabe: "There is really no need for him to apologize, Mr. Grafton, because it's quite plain and you have been aware that he gives that answer when he is not sure, when he can't recall."*
> *Arthur Grafton: "I am likewise quite certain that Mr. Smith makes this answer quite frequently when he is not quite sure what's safe to answer."*[66]

He testified that he ran five separate tests for phenylbutazone, all of which were positive. Cusick and Chinn witnessed, assisted or both with some of the tests, although the extent of their participation was disputed. Two color tests (using Vitali's and Mandelin's reagents), two microcrystal tests (with different reagents) and spectrophotometry tests with acidic and basic buffers were sufficient to call a positive for Bute, the chemist explained.

These five tests were the minimum necessary to confirm the presence of phenylbutazone, according to publications from the Association of Official Racing Chemists (AORC) issued in 1964. Whether the AORC list actually was a recommendation or a requirement for racing chemists was one of many side roads the hearing wandered down, and no one could agree on the answer to that question of semantics. In fact, it took court-ordered discovery for Fuller's legal team to even get to see the secretive AORC lists. About the same time, Harry Peterson, executive secretary of the AORC, went on record in a chemical industry trade journal that the organization had not adopted any analytical methods as "standards,"[67] suggesting that the group's members were on their own with no guidance about best practices in the laboratory.

In 1967, the year before Smith called the "positive" on Dancer's Image, the AORC Standards Committee added a third microcrystal test and thin layer chromatography to the list of required or recommended tests. Smith was unsure whether he had read the 1967 modifications and testified that even if he had, he "had not placed in my mind as important the data to which you refer."[68]

Maurice Cusick and James Chinn also testified that the strong color change in the Vitali test indicated the presence of phenylbutazone. They also testified that they were not experts, and that neither of them understood the spectrophotometer curves or could identify the characteristic crystals Smith said he observed.

Fuller's experts came with impressive credentials, and each one took repeated potshots at Smith and his competence in the lab.

Dr. C.H. Jarboe, head of the Pharmacology Department at the University of Louisville, was critical of all of Smith's test results. He described the black and white photograph of the Vitali positive as "valueless as to establishing color change" in the sample. "If this is evidence," he added, "then it must be negative, for there is no indication of color in this exhibit." He found "no similarity" with known characteristic crystals in the photographs made by Smith, and he dismissed the written statement by the chemist and his assistants that a Mandelin test was positive as proving nothing. This lack of

Dr. C. Harry Jarboe attempts to explain analytical chemistry to the racing commission. *Courtesy of the* Blood-Horse.

documentation, along with conflicting testimony about when the test had been conducted and witnessed by Cusick and Chinn, may not have mattered very much in the final analysis. The experts agreed that the test was old, very nonspecific for Bute or for anything else and of limited usefulness.

The DK-2 alkaline curve obtained on Saturday night after the Derby was worthless, Dr. Jarboe said. "With the alkaline curve dropping off the page, this is unacceptable. It identifies nothing."

Dr. Jarboe's criticism of Smith's tests was supported by other experts: Dr. Gerald Umbreit, analytical chemistry consultant for Greenwood Laboratories in Pennsylvania; Dr. Hans Jaffe, head of the Chemistry Department at the University of Cincinnati and author of a textbook on ultraviolet spectroscopy; and John McDonald, director of the racing chemistry laboratory in Illinois. All of them testified at great length that Smith's tests were not adequate to prove the presence of phenylbutazone.

Fuller's experts also testified that even if performed properly, tests were not specific enough to positively identify phenylbutazone. When asked to identify another substance that would give positive results on all five tests, however, none of them could do so.

There was a welcome break in the expert testimony midway through the hearing, when veterinarians Alex Harthill, Larry Scanlon of Churchill Downs and L.M. Roach of the Kentucky State Racing Commission testified about the condition of Dancer's Image. They all said that the episodes of soreness and soundness attributed to Dancer's Image leading up to the Derby were "consistent" with the administration of Bute, but they also agreed that a horse could have a dramatic recovery from such a condition without receiving any medication at all.

"That a horse was lame on one day and sound the next day doesn't prove he had any medication," Dr. Roach explained.

Lou Cavalaris Jr. and Robert Barnard also testified, but neither of them had anything useful to contribute regarding the disputed chemical tests.

The experts arrayed in support of Kenneth Smith came with credentials at least as impressive as those of Fuller's experts: Lewis Harris, chief chemist for Nebraska; George Jaggard, head of Delare Associates, the lab that tested samples for racing commissions in three states and the Bahamas; and Dr. Francis Ozog, chief racing chemist in Colorado and the man who probably had more experience than anyone else testing for Bute in horse urine. All three men were past presidents of the Association of Official Racing Chemists.

The criticism leveled at Smith and his tests by Fuller's experts focused on the exhibits and documentary evidence. Smith's supporters, on the other hand, emphasized Smith's expertise and the confidence they had in his expert opinion. Like the Churchill Downs stewards, they relied on the word of Smith, an "honorable man…well-regarded and capable in the field of racing chemistry," according to Dr. Jaggard. He said that he could not evaluate the change in color on the basis of Smith's black and white photographs and testified that he would rely instead on the expert conclusion of the person who ran the test.

Reliance on Smith's expert opinion was a theme that ran through the final part of the hearing.

Smith testified that the microcrystal tests he performed all generated crystals that were "typical" or "characteristic" of crystals that phenylbutazone would produce. Smith made a number of color and black and white photographs of the crystals he observed, and he brought the best ones to the commission hearing "for the purpose of demonstrating what I had seen through the microscope."[69] Experts for both sides either were unable to identify any "typical" or "characteristic" crystals in Smith's photographs or refused to even try to do so. They also testified that photographing microcrystals was difficult but possible. Ultimately, two of the commission experts said that they were relying on what Smith said he saw through the microscope rather than what the photographs did or did not show.[70]

Of all the various tests run by Smith after the Derby, the spectrophotometer test performed on the sample buffered with a basic solution was the most definitive for phenylbutazone. It also was the most controversial.

During the stewards' hearing, Smith first testified that the base and acid graphs were "typical" phenylbutazone curves and that they indicated the presence of the drug, but then he began to waffle. Later during the hearing, he contradicted himself and said that he did not rely on the spectrophotometric curves; later still, he said that he could not call the sample positive based on a comparison of his graph with an illustration in a textbook.[71]

The major problem was with the base curve made on Saturday night using the DK-2 machine in the mobile laboratory. Depending on which expert was asked, the problem was either insignificant or very serious. The top of the bell-shaped curve peaked at the correct wavelength for phenylbutazone, but the wavelength corresponding to the minimum absorption point could not be read because the graph ran off the page. Commission experts generally found Smith's graphs indicative of phenylbutazone; Fuller's experts were less sure about that.

Dr. Ozog, who found serious problems with the laboratory expertise of Smith, eventually found a positive result for phenylbutazone in one of the UV curves by making a series of speculative adjustments and assumptions to correct apparent testing errors by Smith.

Of all the experts who testified during the hearing, the most intriguing was Lewis Harris, the Nebraska chemist who performed the only independent tests on the urine collected from Dancer's Image. Smith mailed the sample to Harris on Sunday after the Derby, but it did not arrive until the following Tuesday. Around the time that Wathen Knebelkamp was making his announcement to the press at Churchill Downs, Harris was running the first Vitali test on the sample he received from Harris. The result for that test was a "very faint positive or a very weak positive."[72] When Harris repeated the other tests that Smith had run, however, all the results were negative. Harris repeated the series of tests, as good laboratory procedure dictates, and he got the same negative results. Harris also subjected the sample to thin layer chromatography, a procedure Smith had not used, and that test also was negative.[73]

The sample, it seemed, was as contradictory as much of the testimony, showing results both positive and negative for Bute. However, the consensus of the experts who testified at the hearing was that a positive result on all of Smith's tests was the minimum required for a positive finding, suggesting that Harris's tests did not support Smith's conclusion.

So how, then, did Harris wind up as a witness for the commission?

During his deposition, Smith said that the sample he sent to Harris was urine from which all or most of the phenylbutazone had been extracted during the Saturday and Sunday tests. This was the first time that Fuller's attorneys had heard anything about Harris. There was enough of the drug remaining to give the weak positive on the Vitali test, Smith speculated, but not enough to register on any of the other tests. Even if this might have explained the negative results in Harris's tests, the explanation raised other questions: Why would Smith send an extracted sample to Harris for the sole purpose of confirming the presence of phenylbutazone? Why did Smith tell commission chairman Egger that Harris had found a faint positive but that the sample had been badly decomposed, which Harris later denied? Why were the Harris tests not disclosed to Fuller for almost six months?

In the end, with nearly three thousand pages of conflicting and contradictory testimony to choose from, the commissioners could find support for just about any finding they wished to make regarding Dancer's Image and Bute. It might even have been tempting to simply count the pages of testimony supporting each side, or weigh the transcripts, and decide on that basis.

Ultimately, the racing commission chose to uphold the single finding of fact made by the stewards, that Dancer's Image won the Derby with phenylbutazone in his system,[74] and then add some findings of its own.

The commissioners determined as facts, among other things:

- that Dancer's Image finished first in the Kentucky Derby (everyone already knew he was the best horse that day);
- that urine was collected from the horse and tested by Smith and his assistants;
- that all the initial test results were positive for phenylbutazone (relying on Smith's testimony and an expansive reading of testimony from the commission experts);
- that the positive results were confirmed by a second series of tests conducted by Smith (run on Tuesday, after the announcement that Dancer's Image was the horse which tested positive for Bute);
- that Dancer's Image suffered from serious ankle problems during the week before the Derby and that phenylbutazone was the only medication that could have alleviated the horse's soreness;
- that the "use of phenylbutazone contributed to the sound condition of Dancer's Image" when he raced in the Derby;
- that phenylbutazone affects the speed of a horse by allowing the animal to race to its full potential; and
- that the presence of any trace of phenylbutazone in the urine sample collected from Dancer's Image showed that the drug's "administration affected the health and speed of the horse by enabling him to run racing sound."

Of all the commission's findings, the last was especially problematic. By cobbling together anecdotal evidence that Dancer's Image was sore on Thursday and racing sound on Saturday, the conclusion that only phenylbutazone could have caused such a "dramatic" change in the horse's condition and the positive test results attributed to Smith, the commissioners seemed to be stating as fact that the horse received a dose of Bute on Wednesday evening or early on Thursday. There was no way to know that, however, and veterinary testimony during the hearing unanimously held that a sore horse could recover without any medication. At best, Smith's tests showed the presence of Bute but not the amount. Even if the tests were reliable, and testimony about that was far from conclusive, Smith said that he could not judge the amount of Bute in the sample because his tests were qualitative and not quantitative.[75]

(George Jaggard was willing to make an educated guess about that. He estimated that Smith's test results showed a concentration of about 150 micrograms of phenylbutazone per milliliter of urine, which he thought could result from a normal dose of Bute about twenty-four hours before the urine collection. How he made this guess is not clear, since he also testified that he did not rely on Smith's exhibits. That timetable also does not account

The "official" winner of the 1968 Kentucky Derby still was in doubt at the end of the year. © Courier-Journal. *Reprinted with permission.*

for the improvement of the horse's ankle on Thursday, more than forty-eight hours before the Derby.)

Having determined that Dancer's Image won the Kentucky Derby with traces of Bute in his system, the commissioners affirmed the redistribution of the purse. They added that their ruling did not affect the order of finish. The importance of this addendum would not become apparent for months.

Fuller put together an impressive record in the boxing ring, winning fifty of fifty-five fights, and there was some talk that he might have been good enough to box in the Olympics. Now he was zero for two against the stewards and the racing commission. Fuller's next step was out of the administrative arena and into court.

***

Administrative agencies like the Kentucky State Racing Commission are given substantial deference when it comes to fact finding. The commissioners were the ones who saw and heard the witnesses during the hearing and should be in the best position to assess the credibility of the testimony. Courts also assume, rightly or wrongly, that a specialized agency has expertise that a general purpose court does not. Anyone who feels shortchanged or wronged by a commission decision has the right to appeal the ruling to Franklin Circuit Court, but that did not mean that Fuller would get a new hearing. Another bite of the apple was out of the question.

Judicial review of an administrative decision is limited to three very narrow areas: whether the commission acted beyond its power, whether the decision was obtained through fraud and whether there was "substantial evidence" to support the commissioners' factual findings. It is rare, indeed, for a court to overturn an administrative order.

Chairman Egger and the other commissioners made several very specific findings of fact, but the only one that mattered—the only one that ever mattered—was that phenylbutazone and/or a derivative was present in the urine of Dancer's Image following the Kentucky Derby. The only question before the Franklin Circuit Court was whether there was "substantial evidence" in the record to support that assertion. If there was such evidence, Judge Henry Meigs could not substitute his own conclusions for those of the commission, no matter how erroneous he thought the commission might be. On the other hand, if there was no substantial evidence supporting the racing commission decision in the record, Judge Meigs could toss out the ruling and, with it, the alleged medication rule violation.

Unlike everyone else—Fuller and Cavalaris, a small law firm's worth of attorneys, the stewards, the racing commissioners, Kenneth Smith—Judge Meigs did not have a dog in the Dancer's Image fight. Throughout the lengthy administrative hearings and the ensuing litigation, he was the only person who reviewed all the evidence and evaluated Kenneth Smith's reliability as a witness without any interest in the outcome. When Judge Meigs did that, he found both the chemist and the evidence lacking.

The stewards apparently pressured Kenneth Smith into a decision when he may have had some doubts and then simply took his "positive" result at face value. The only purpose of the stewards' hearing was to lay blame, not to question the integrity of the test. That was what stewards had done for as long as there had been rules and racing chemists, and that was what they did in the Dancer's Image case. After the test results were announced to the public, the stewards had an obvious, if unstated, interest in saving face and preserving the reputation of their racing chemist.

Members of the racing commission, likewise, had an interest in protecting the integrity of Smith, a commission hire who never had been challenged like this during many years on the job. Without a reliable racing chemist, the Rules of Racing were nothing more than words on paper. Fuller's attorneys felt that the stewards and the commissioners all had prejudged the case by their reliance on Smith, and their deposition testimony and some posthearing public statements seemed to support the accusations.[76]

Hovering above both hearings was the "good of racing" and the potential threat posed to the sport by a seemingly sore loser like Peter Fuller.

Judge Meigs gave the stewards and the commissioners the benefit of the doubt. Despite "misunderstanding, misconception, and mischance" that "attended every unraveling thread of this case," Judge Meigs concluded that "the Chairman and members of the Racing Commission conducted themselves at all times in a manner bespeaking the highest fidelity to the ideals of fairness and impartiality."[77]

Judge Meigs was not so kind to Kenneth Smith.

Starting with the proposition that "only the conclusion of a professional chemist—or chemists—will support a determination either way—positive or negative" about the presence of Bute in a urine sample, Judge Meigs disregarded nearly all the expert testimony that took up most of the hearing time. Some of that testimony supported Smith, some of it called his competence and conclusions into question, but all of it was what Judge Meigs characterized as "opinion based upon the opinions or conclusions—as opposed to facts—of another expert witness, the rankest form of hearsay evidence."[78]

Only one independent racing chemist had actually tested the urine collected from Dancer's Image, Lewis Harris in Nebraska, and both sides argued that his findings supported their positions.

That left only the testimony of Smith and the exhibits he produced to bolster his conclusion as the basis for the commission determination that Dancer's Image won the Kentucky Derby with Bute in his system. That evidence was not substantial enough to satisfy Judge Meigs.

> *Kenneth Smith's oral testimony standing alone qualified as admissible expert opinion evidence, based on tests, conclusions and inferences a professional chemist is competent to make or draw. When he attempted to buttress his opinions by the introduction of demonstrative, objective data he destroyed the probative value and weight of his own opinions and his scientific brethren confirmed the kill. With the sole exception of his 'spectrophotometric curve at pH two to three,' the demonstrative effect of each of Smith's tests either directly contradicts his stated opinion of what he had determined, displays something else altogether, portrays nothing recognizable to him or to any other chemical expert, or, as the elaborate explanation of another witness would have it, shows that his spectrophotometer either malfunctioned or its measurements were misread.*

Upon all the evidence in the voluminous record the Commission has made a finding and order for which support can only rest on the testimony of Kenneth Smith. Most of the rest of the testimony was either inadmissible, or reflects opinions unsupported by facts. Smith's testimony, supplemented and explained by wholly inconclusive and often contradictory testimony and exhibits, loses all probative force. Thus stripped away, such evidence is wholly lacking in substance and relevant consequence, having the fitness to induce conviction in the minds of reasonable men. It cannot be accepted as adequate to support the conclusion reached by the Commission.[79]

Some twenty months after he crossed the finish line in front of Forward Pass and a dozen other three-year-olds, Dancer's Image again was in line to receive the winner's share of the Derby purse. The purse distribution still was not final, though. One more court had to weigh in on the outcome of the race.

***

In June 1972, more than four years after Dancer's Image apparently won the Kentucky Derby, the state's highest court reversed Judge Meigs and decided in favor of the Kentucky State Racing Commission.[80] Judge Meigs ruled for Fuller after tossing out as inadmissible most of the expert testimony from the commission hearing and finding what was left—the testimony of Kenneth Smith—unbelievable. The Kentucky Court of Appeals took a different approach. The court did not rule on the admissibility of evidence at the hearing. Instead, the justices considered the entire record.

The court acknowledged that there were "numerous contradictions and even contradictions of contradictions throughout this entire record." Nevertheless, the court said, the commissioners who saw and heard the witnesses testify were better situated to "consider the credibility of the witnesses; and to determine the weight as between conflicting statements of witnesses or even a single witness." On that basis, there was "substantial evidence supporting the findings and rulings of the Kentucky State Racing Commission."

In effect, although the court of appeals did not come out and say so, the commissioners had permission to believe an unbelievable witness.

Chapter 8

THE HOLY GRAIL

The decision by the Kentucky Court of Appeals was a hard body blow that left Peter Fuller reeling both financially and emotionally. He had been cut out of the Kentucky Derby purse distribution, apparently for good; the original syndication plans for Dancer's Image had failed to materialize after the medication positive was announced; and legal bills fueled by years of litigation were piling up at an alarming rate. His horse had won the most sought-after prize in racing, lost it in hearing rooms, scored a victory in court and then lost again in another court. Fuller was like an unwilling rider on a bizarre roller coaster that reaches the heights of the rattling contraption only to face a stomach-churning drop, over and over.

He was down but not out—not yet. Amazingly, there still was some fight left in the former boxer. He had one shot remaining, and his attorneys set their sights on a technical knockout. Success depended on whether the rules of racing really meant what they said.

Almost from the moment the positive drug test result on Dancer's Image was announced, the press and just about everyone else talked about the horse's Derby "disqualification." It made sense at the time to do so. Everyone understood what being "disqualified" meant, and it relieved sports writers of the bothersome task of starting each story about the race with a lengthy explanation of what actually was going on in Kentucky. In fact, though, Dancer's Image still was the winner of the 1968 Kentucky Derby, thanks to a peculiar quirk of the rules in effect in Kentucky on the first Saturday in May 1968.

When the Kentucky Stage Racing Commission found as a matter of law that the urine sample taken from Dancer's Image contained traces of phenylbutazone or a derivative of the prohibited medication, the ruling established a violation of Kentucky Rule of Racing 14.04. A few paragraphs further along in the rule book, Rule 14.06 required that Dancer's Image be cut out of the purse distribution for the Kentucky Derby. That cost Peter Fuller $122,600; the rules were crystal clear on the outcome.

The rules were equally clear on another salient point, however. The order of finish in the 1968 Kentucky Derby was not changed by the positive test result. The racing commission affirmed this in its order on January 6, 1969, stating: "Under the Kentucky Rules of Racing which governed the Derby race on May 4, 1968, the foregoing ruling does not affect the order of finish. The betting on the race and the payment of parimutuel tickets thereon should in no way be affected." Much as the members of the racing commission might have wanted to, they did not, and could not, declare Forward Pass the "winner" of the 1968 Kentucky Derby.

The language of both the rule entry and the commission ruling were necessary to avoid confusion among the hundreds of thousands of bettors who wagered on the outcome of the Derby. The race was declared "OFFICIAL" by the placing judges at Churchill Downs a few minutes after Dancer's Image carried Fuller's silks across the finish line ahead of everyone else. The decision of the placing judges, according to the rules, was final. Winning tickets on Dancer's Image were cashed (or possibly saved as souvenirs); tickets with favored Forward Pass as the winner were discarded as worthless. Changing the order of finish by taking Dancer's Image down and placing Forward Pass first some eight months after the fact would create a bettor's nightmare.

Common sense might have suggested that the horse that received the winner's share of the Derby purse also was the "winner" of the race in every other context. The rules should have made that clear if that was the intent. They did not, and the omission created a loophole large enough for Peter Fuller and his attorneys to ride a horse through. The dilemma for the commission became what to do with Dancer's Image once it was obvious that Fuller was not going to fold up his tent and go away after the court of appeals decision.

The rules were silent about the postrace status of a winning horse following a positive drug test. The plain language of the rules left only one conclusion, though, and it was a strange one. Calumet Farm's Forward Pass was awarded first-place money because the racing commission said so, but Peter Fuller still had a legitimate claim to have Dancer's Image recognized as the "winner" of the Derby because the commission ruling specifically did not alter the order of finish. And Dancer's Image undeniably crossed the finish line first. A Churchill Downs crowd estimated at 100,000 and millions more racing fans glued to their television screens all could attest to that.

Spectators watching the race that day also saw Kentucky governor Louis B. Nunn hand the impressive gold winner's trophy to Fuller. He subsequently relinquished the hardware for engraving, a decision he would come to regret. When news of the positive drug test broke three days after the race, Churchill Downs officials consigned the Derby trophy to Lemon's Jewelers in Louisville for safekeeping in the company vault.

Four years later, with the original order of finish confirmed by the stewards, the racing commission and the Kentucky Court of Appeals, Fuller asked Churchill Downs president Lynn Stone to deliver the Derby trophy to him. In a letter to Stone, dated July 17, 1972, attorney Arthur Grafton reminded Stone that Dancer's Image had finished first in the Derby. Because everyone agreed that the order of finish in the race had survived various commission and court rulings, Fuller was entitled to his trophy.

Soon afterward, representatives of Calumet Farm made a similar request to Churchill Downs for the Derby trophy on behalf of Forward Pass, based on the court ruling.

Churchill Downs had managed to stay out of the controversy, at least officially, but now track officials were faced with competing claims for the same trophy. Whatever the decision, another round of litigation was almost a sure thing. Calumet's request had logic and a check for the winner's share of the Derby purse on its side, but Fuller's claim relied on an interpretation of the rules that, on its face at least, was not unreasonable.

Churchill Downs never claimed any financial interest in the ultimate outcome of the disputed Derby, for good reason. There was no doubt that the contested purse money and the gold trophy would go to someone other than the track when the owners and lawyers finally ran out of steam. The only question was, who? The purse distribution finally had been resolved in court, and rather than make a decision about the trophy, Churchill Downs officials quickly passed the buck to the racing commission. The track's Application for Ruling requested an official decision about what to do with the trophy.

It was a shrewd move.

The commission already had awarded the winner's share of the purse to Forward Pass, and a similar ruling about the trophy was likely and probably expected. Either way, though, the track was off the hook.

Even if Churchill Downs had no financial interest in the matter, it would be disingenuous to claim that the track had no interest at all in whether Peter

Fuller or Calumet Farm eventually was awarded the Derby trophy. There was the matter of saving face.

In court pleadings, the track would claim a

> *vital interest in the maintenance of the highest degree of honesty and integrity in Thoroughbred racing in Kentucky for the ultimate good of the sport itself…Churchill Downs believes that the public's confidence would be badly shaken and the image of Thoroughbred racing in Kentucky would be tarnished if the Kentucky Derby trophy should be awarded to the owner of a horse which the Commission and the Court have declared ineligible to participate in the purse by reason of having been medicated with a forbidden drug in direct violation of the Commission Rules.*

It was a backhanded way of saying that both Churchill Downs and the commissioners making the decision would be laughingstocks if Peter Fuller actually wound up with the Derby trophy.

There still was a glimmer of hope in the Dancer's Image camp, though, even if the racing commission's decision appeared to be a foregone conclusion. Republican governor Louie B. Nunn had been defeated by a Democrat, Wendell H. Ford, in the 1971 gubernatorial election, and when Ford took office, he appointed an entirely new commission. Fuller and his attorneys would make their argument about the trophy to commissioners who had not been involved in the purse decision. A new slate of commissioners might not help, but it certainly would not hurt.

On October 19, 1972, there was a "special called meeting" of the racing commission at Evans Industries in Lexington. Chairman William H. May and Vice-Chairman Robert C. Stilz were present, along with Commissioners Charles Nuckols Jr. and George E. Evans Jr. The fifth member of the commission, William F. Lucas, participated in the meeting by telephone. The meeting was brief, generating less than two pages of transcribed notes. The only substantive issue was the Derby trophy.[81]

The commissioners decided unanimously that "the 1968 Gold Cup Kentucky Derby Trophy shall be awarded to Calumet Farm, the owner of Forward Pass and that the horse, Forward Pass should hereafter be considered the winner of the 1968 Kentucky Derby in all respects and for all intents and purposes."

Having answered the question about disposition of the Derby trophy, the commission seemed unsure about what to do with the information.

News of the "special" meeting was released to the press a week later, on October 27, and the next day, notice of the "Official Ruling" appeared on page 2 of the *Daily Racing Form*. However, notes from the meeting were not transcribed in the official minutes of the racing commission until November 13, almost a month after the meeting at Evans Industries and nineteen days after notice of the ruling first appeared in the press.

Adding to the confusion, the commission met again on December 2 at the Versailles, Kentucky home of Vice-Chairman Stilz. Commissioners May, Nuckols and Evans showed up in person; Lukas again participated by telephone. Stilz's motion that the October 19 order, giving the Derby trophy to Calumet Farm, be "re-adopted, ratified and confirmed" was passed unanimously, and for good measure, the commission also "ratified and confirmed" the January 6, 1969 commission order that redistributed the Derby purse.

The "special" meetings at odd locations away from the commission office, apparently with no notice to Fuller or his attorneys, the premature release of the commission decision to the press and the delay in transcribing the meeting notes to the official minutes all might have been the innocent bumbling of an agency uncomfortable with the quasijudicial role thrust upon it. Or they might have been conscious efforts to obfuscate things. It did not really matter. Fuller and his attorneys were left in a quandary either way.

Fuller wanted to appeal the racing commission ruling to the Franklin County Circuit Court, where Judge Henry Meigs still was on the bench. Judge Meigs had reversed the racing commission on the purse distribution question and might be a sympathetic ear. But to get the case before Judge Meigs, an appeal had to be filed within a very short timeframe proscribed by Kentucky law. The problem was that Fuller's attorneys had no idea when the filing clock started ticking.

It made perfect sense that the order approved at the October 19 special meeting was a final ruling that triggered the clock for filing a timely appeal, but Fuller never had received notice of that order. He and his attorneys learned of the adverse ruling only when it was reported in the *Daily Racing Form* on October 28. Reasoning that it was better to be safe than sorry, an appeal of the adverse ruling was filed by Fuller's attorneys on November 4. It was a decision that was sensible and prudent—and ultimately wrong.

At a hearing on March 30, 1973, attorney Arthur Grafton told Judge Meigs that the Kentucky State Racing Commission had no authority to award the Derby trophy to anyone other than Peter Fuller. The nomination form for the 1968 Kentucky Derby included a provision that the Kentucky Rules of Racing would govern any disputes, and Grafton reminded Judge Meigs that the rules in effect at the time limited the authority of the commission to a redistribution of the purse. Any action beyond that, Grafton argued, such as awarding the trophy to Calumet Farm or declaring Forward Pass the winner of the Derby for "all intents and purposes," was beyond the scope of the commission's authority.

Across the courtroom sat political heavyweight Bert T. Combs, a former governor of Kentucky, and attorney John E. Tarrant, general counsel for Churchill Downs. Both men felt that Fuller's attempt to claim the Derby trophy was a serious threat to the most famous horse race in the world and to the reputation of Churchill Downs.

Not surprisingly, Tarrant disagreed with Grafton's strict interpretation of the Rules of Racing. In Tarrant's view, the rules, at most, established a floor for the racing commission's authority, not a ceiling.

"The rules of the commission are not perfect, legally stated documents," he told the court. "But the authority of the commission is not circumscribed by the rules it adopts. The statute says that the commission has complete jurisdiction over racing in Kentucky."

Judge Meigs already had demonstrated that he had no misgivings about challenging the racing commission, and Fuller's appeal gave him another opportunity to do so. He did not take it, though, because he did not need to. Fuller and his attorneys had been hoping for a technical knockout, but Judge Meigs delivered one of his own. He tossed out the appeal without ever reaching the merits of Fuller's argument that he was the rightful owner of the Derby trophy.

Although the racing commission met and decided to award the trophy to Calumet Farm on October 19, the ruling was not entered into the agency's official record until November 13. For twenty-five days, the commission decision apparently floated in some sort of legal limbo, written down in the informal minutes of the special meeting and released to the press but not yet made a part of the official record. When Fuller's appeal was filed on November 4, there still was no "final determination of the matters in controversy" to be appealed, according to Judge Meigs. By the time the commission ruling finally made its way into the official agency record on November 13, Fuller's attorneys reasonably thought they already had a valid appeal moving through the system and they took no more action. The ten-day filing period that started when the ruling finally was entered into the official record passed without any new pleadings.

"Appellant (Fuller) has failed to perfect a timely appeal," Judge Meigs said, "therefore the court lacks jurisdiction to do other than dismiss the attempt."

In a bizarre series of events that would have made the residents of Lewis Carroll's Wonderland feel right at home, Fuller's appeal managed to be both too early and too late.

"There are no rights left to declare," Judge Meigs wrote in an April 13, 1973 memo opinion, dismissing the appeal. "Peter Fuller has had his day in court; it is regrettable that it had to be such a sorry day."

***

Five years, two months, two weeks and a day after the 1968 Kentucky Derby was run with Dancer's Image the apparent winner, Churchill Downs president Lynn Stone made the eighty-mile drive from Churchill Downs to Calumet Farm on the west side of Lexington. Calumet is the epitome of a Thoroughbred horse farm, rolling acres of manicured bluegrass, immaculate red and white barns, miles of pristine white plank fences. As Stone made his way slowly along the tree-lined drive on the blazing hot July afternoon, Forward Pass grazed in one of the paddocks.

Calumet Farm's eight Kentucky Derby trophies are on display at the Kentucky Horse Park. *Courtesy of the Kentucky Horse Park.*

The Holy Grail

Waiting in an office rich with leather furniture, wood paneled walls and paintings of famous horses were farm manager Melvin Cinnamon and office manager Mrs. Margaret Glass—Maggie to just about everyone who knew her. Mrs. Lucille Markey, owner of Calumet, was absent, confined by illness to her home in Saratoga, New York. Stone offered to travel to Saratoga, but Mrs. Markey said that it was not necessary. The trophy Stone was carrying, a gold cup topped by a statuette of a racehorse and jockey, belonged in Kentucky with Calumet's seven other Kentucky Derby trophies.

Before Stone arrived, Maggie Glass had retrieved the other Derby trophies from the Calumet vault and lined them up like seven gold-armored soldiers on a table. It was an embarrassment of riches, already the most impressive grouping of Derby hardware on the planet, and Stone was about to add an eighth gold cup to the collection. He handed the trophy first to Glass and then repeated the presentation to Cinnamon. It was a surreal scene, far removed from the raucous winner's circle ceremonies when Peter Fuller accepted the same gold cup from the Kentucky governor on May 4, 1968.

The longest Derby finally was over. Now the only concern for Maggie Glass was how to make room for the newest addition among Calumet's 479 other race trophies in the vault.

"We'll just have to squeeze it in," she said. "Maybe we'll have to rearrange a few to make room. But I couldn't think of a nicer arrangement to have to make."[82]

Chapter 9

THE USUAL SUSPECTS

Hearings, lawsuits and thousands of pages of testimony, at best, showed that Kenneth Smith's tests met the minimum legal standard necessary to establish that Dancer's Image won the Derby with the help of a prohibited medication. At worst, they demonstrated serious shortcomings in a system for drug testing and rule enforcement that no one had seriously challenged before.

But the questions that really intrigued everyone—What happened? Who did it? Why?—all went unanswered. After the stewards' hearing, those questions were not even asked very often, at least not officially. The rules did not require a "who" or a "why," only an official chemist with a positive test result in his hand, and attention quickly shifted to the competence of Smith and the reliability of his tests. Finding someone to blame might even have been counterproductive by compromising arguments that Smith's testing was wrong or was at least fatally unreliable. Conclusive evidence of a culprit would establish, rather than eliminate, charges that Dancer's Image had been medicated with Bute prior to the Derby.

More than forty years later, the mystery about events surrounding that first Saturday in May still lingers. Without a confession from someone, very unlikely at this point, any attempt to "solve" the Dancer's Image mystery necessarily involves the rankest of speculation.

***

Lawyers often make alternative arguments that seem to be at odds with each other. At the stewards' hearing, Fuller's attorneys claimed that there was no phenylbutazone in the urine sample collected from Dancer's Image, and that any chemical tests that seemed to indicate otherwise either were wrong or were so unreliable that the results could not be believed. Or—and this is the alternative argument—it was possible that Sample 3956U was not urine from Dancer's Image at all. Someone, either intentionally or inadvertently, could have switched samples so that the positive test results attributed to Dancer's Image did not belong to him at all.

Proving that Sample 3956U actually was urine from a horse that was not Dancer's Image would have ended the dispute. The winner's share of the purse would go into Peter Fuller's bank account and the gold trophy would be on his mantel. But the chain of custody from Dancer's Image to testing veterinarian Sidney Turner to supervising veterinarian L.M. Roach to lab technician James Chinn to chief chemist Kenneth Smith was practically unassailable. When the commission hearing rolled around, the switched-sample argument had been abandoned and with it one opportunity to search for chicanery.[83]

A quirk in the rules seriously hampered the claim that even if the urine did come from Dancer's Image, Sample 3956U contained no phenylbutazone. Good lab practice, not to mention common sense when a race as important as the Kentucky Derby is involved, dictates that a portion of any positive sample should be retained for subsequent testing. The rules did not require that, however, and Smith either used up the entire sample or discarded what was left when he finished his tests. Fuller and his attorneys were either way deprived the opportunity for independent testing that might have confirmed their suspicions that Sample 3956U contained no traces of phenylbutazone. Lacking a sample, and initially unaware that Smith had sent a sample to an outside laboratory, the fallback position for Fuller's attorneys was that Smith's test results were either wrong or so flawed that they could not be taken seriously. These related arguments eventually were dismissed by the Kentucky State Racing Commission, with a nod from the court of appeals.

Aside from the many technical challenges to Smith's testing that were coming from Fuller's legal team, there was circumstantial evidence that Dancer's Image had not raced with the assistance of Bute on Derby Day.

Prior to the Derby, Dancer's Image had won a dozen times at six different tracks, three of them in Canada and three in the United States. No horse in the Derby field had won more races or, by extension, had been tested for prohibited medications as often as Dancer's Image. Despite a career plagued by ankle problems, the horse never had tested positive before. He won impressively without Bute prior to the Derby, against some of the horses in the Derby field, making the postrace positive a striking anomaly in an otherwise clean record.

Also, everyone acknowledged that Dancer's Image received an oral dose of phenylbutazone on the Sunday before the Derby, four grams administered by Dr. Harthill and witnessed by Cavalaris. The therapeutic effect of that dose was long gone by the Derby, and six days should have been sufficient for traces of the drug to clear the horse's system. It was the first time the horse ever had received the anti-inflammatory drug, and it made him sick the next day with colic and diarrhea. These were side effects often associated with the medication. The gastrointestinal upsets did not occur again prior to the Derby, however—circumstantial evidence that the horse never received a similar dose of Bute closer in time to the Derby.

Finally, Dancer's Image had been an iron horse throughout his career. Thanks to ongoing care from his trainer and his own remarkable resilience, Dancer's Image seldom missed a workout or a race. He seemed to thrive on the long gallops that were the cornerstone of his conditioning, and in this light, the rapid improvement in his troublesome right ankle on Thursday before the Derby seems less sinister.

The commissioners determined that phenylbutazone was the "medication of choice" for sore ankles like those of Dancer's Image, that no other medication had "the dramatic effects of this drug in the treatment of such a condition" and that the Thursday improvement in the horse's condition was "consistent with the use…of phenylbutazone in veterinary medicine."[84] From these statements, the commissioners made an evidentiary leap from "could" to "did" and determined as a matter of fact that Bute contributed to the Derby win.

Dr. Alex Harthill, the only veterinarian who treated Dancer's Image at Churchill Downs, was not so positive about the causal link put forward by the commission. He testified that the large dose of Azium he administered to Dancer's Image before the horse galloped on Thursday could have contributed to the recovery, and that in his experience, horses with sore ankles sometimes get better without any medication at all.[85] Other veterinarians shared this opinion.

Picking out bits and pieces of contradictory testimony offered over many days, the racing commission determined that Dancer's Image won a Bute-assisted Kentucky Derby. The proof certainly did not rise to the "beyond a reasonable doubt" standard required for a conviction in a criminal trial and probably not even to the "more likely than not" standard needed to win a civil lawsuit. All that was required, though, was "substantial evidence" to support the commission ruling, and Kentucky's highest court determined that there was enough evidence for that.

Even assuming that Kenneth Smith and the racing commission got it right, the ruling cast no light at all on who might have given Bute to Dancer's Image or why.

***

A spouse almost always is the primary suspect when a husband or wife is murdered, and the trainer likewise is the first person authorities look to when a racehorse tests positive for a prohibited medication. Even when there is no evidence that a trainer actually did anything to break the rules, racing's "trainer responsibility rule" holds the trainer ultimately responsible for the condition of the horses in his care. It was on this basis, rather than any evidence that he had been involved in slipping Bute to Dancer's Image before the Derby, that Lou Cavalaris drew a thirty-day suspension from the Churchill Downs stewards.

It is a tough rule, especially under the circumstances surrounding the Dancer's Image controversy. Following the racing commission's logic, Dancer's Image must have received a second dose of Bute late on Wednesday or early the next day, which in turn brought about his dramatic improvement on Thursday and his ability to race soundly on Saturday. That timeline would mirror the horse's improved condition on Monday before the Derby after his first dose of Bute the day before.

Even if Cavalaris had wanted to medicate Dancer's Image on Wednesday, though, he could not have done it. The trainer was out of town, tending to his stable in Canada during the middle of the week.

Through it all, Cavalaris vehemently denied any wrongdoing to the stewards and to anyone else who would listen, and a nearly spotless disciplinary record backed him up. During more than two decades as a trainer, Cavalaris had never been suspended, and he had been fined only twice for minor offenses: twenty-five dollars for entering an ineligible horse at Woodbine and another twenty-five dollars for failing to name a jockey for a horse he trained.

It also was clear that Cavalaris knew the risks involved with dosing Dancer's Image with Bute too close to a race. Dancer's Image appeared to thrive on work despite his iffy ankles, and the original plan had been to enter the horse in the Derby Trial on Tuesday, then run him back in the Derby four days later. That plan was abandoned after Dr. Harthill administered the oral dose of Bute on Sunday, just two days before the Derby Trial. The horse did not start in that race, and it defies reason to think that Cavalaris would take a chance with more Bute close in time to the most important race in the world when he knew the winner would be tested.

While Cavalaris was on the road during Derby Week, responsibility for the care and training of Dancer's Image fell to assistant trainer Robert Barnard. He also denied any involvement, and there was no evidence to suggest otherwise. Barnard, like Cavalaris, was suspended for thirty days due to his status as de facto trainer for Dancer's Image during Cavalaris's absences. There also was no evidence that Barnard even knew that phenylbutazone might help Dancer's Image. Barnard did not arrive in Louisville until Monday before the Derby, and Cavalaris apparently did not tell him about the medication administered by Dr. Harthill a day earlier.

Peter Fuller was the person who stood to benefit the most from a win in the Derby. A multimillion-dollar syndication for Dancer's Image was a reasonable expectation with a victory, and the prestige associated with owning a Derby winner was incalculable. Fuller was at the center of the Bute controversy because he owned Dancer's Image, but he had almost no day-to-day control, either of the horse before the race or of the legal wranglings afterward.

More compelling than his lack of opportunity, though, was the man himself. Alvan Tufts Fuller was a self-made man of honor, and Peter Fuller was his father's son, through and through. Winning the Derby with help from a prohibited medication would be a tainted victory for Fuller, whether he got caught, and there was no suggestion that hitting below the belt was in his nature. There also was no pressure from Fuller to run a sore horse.

"Regardless of the family and friends I brought with me from Boston," he told Cavalaris prior to the Derby, "if Dancer's Image is not perfectly all right and able to do his best, I would rather he didn't run."[86]

***

Crank letters left Peter Fuller concerned about a possible backlash from his gift to the Reverend Martin Luther King's widow after the Governor's Gold Cup, concerned enough to request additional security for Dancer's Image at Churchill Downs. The request was denied. After he got word of the positive drug test, Fuller was critical of security at the track.

"I don't want to poke holes in racing," he said, "but this kind of security is enough to make a cat laugh."[87] Protection for Dancer's Image, he said, "was an old fella sitting in a chair and asleep."[88] Fuller later tempered his comments a bit, but the question he raised about security for Derby horses was a valid one.

On Tuesday after the Derby, late at night, *Courier-Journal* reporters Billy Reed and Jim Bolus drove onto the Churchill Downs backstretch with a valid press pass and parked their car next to the Harthill Barn. The "old fella" they found guarding Dancer's Image and the other horses in Barn 24 was asleep in a tack room and almost impossible to rouse.

"We walked down the shedrow, found the stall, opened the door, and petted Dancer's Image," Reed recalled. "Then we went back and tried to wake up the guard. We stopped at a White Castle on the way to the race track and we even popped the paper bag without waking him up."[89]

Even if security in the barn area was not as tight as it might have been, odds are long that an outsider angered by Fuller's support for the civil rights movement actually tampered with Dancer's Image. An intruder would have to know about the horse's ankle problems; know that Bute might help the condition; acquire the proper dose of the drug; gain access to the stable area, probably in the dead of night; locate Barn 24; slip past whatever security happened to be there; find the stall where Dancer's Image was housed; administer the drug to a fractious, one-thousand-pound Thoroughbred; and steal away unnoticed. It is a possible but highly improbable, chain of events.

Then for the scheme to work, Dancer's Image would have to win the Kentucky Derby, the drug would have to be found in a postrace test, the horse would have to be disqualified and Fuller's appeals would have to be denied. It is an insanely complicated scenario that required sophisticated planning along with knowledge of racing and pharmacology. Letter-writing racists, who tend not to be not intellectual giants in the first place, probably are not the best candidates to pull off something like that. A far simpler plan for an outsider who wanted to hurt Fuller would be to poison Dancer's Image or drug the horse so he would lose, rather than win, the Derby.

Whether Fuller's gift to Mrs. King ruffled the feathers of someone on the inside is another matter entirely.

Fuller later recalled a conversation he had with Paul Mellon, a successful Thoroughbred owner and philanthropist, about the Bute controversy: "Peter, you shouldn't have mixed politics and racing."[90] The company line, though, was clear—there was no pressure for anyone to do anything untoward.

Even if not directly related to Fuller's gift, the handling of the controversy angered some very important people. Mrs. Gene Markey, whose Calumet

Farm had amassed more Derby history than any other stable, was adamant that Calumet's devil's red and blue silks would not be seen on a track in Kentucky until Forward Pass was declared the winner of the Derby.[91]

Sometime after things had cooled down a little, Fuller contacted Kenneth Smith and asked the chemist directly whether anyone had tried to influence his conclusions. There had been no pressure from Mrs. Markey or from anyone else, Smith told Fuller.[92] Undue influence is hard to prove. There certainly was no evidence to refute the company line.

*****

That leaves Dr. Alex Harthill and the "other matters" hinted at by the stewards in May 1968 but not made public until months later. In a case filled with puzzles, the controversial veterinarian almost certainly tops the list.

Dr. Harthill's stockpile of veterinary drugs included phenylbutazone, and he had easy and uncontrolled access to Dancer's Image throughout Derby Week. The horse was in the same barn as the veterinarian's office, just a short stroll down the shed row, and Dr. Harthill was the treating veterinarian. And, as the racing commissioners might have said, Dr. Harthill enjoyed a reputation among horsemen that was "consistent" with a Kentucky Derby tainted by a medication controversy.

He also admitted to tampering with feed for Dancer's Image, although the "salting" incident, as it came to be known, was part of a harebrained plan that took shape two days after the Derby rather than two days before the race. Dr. Harthill and a friend who had horses in a barn adjacent to Barn 24, trainer Doug Davis Jr., eventually were offered a choice by the racing commission for their participation in the bizarre scheme: accept a $500 fine or a thirty-day suspension. Both Dr. Harthill and Davis chose the fine.[93]

It happened like this:

Lou Cavalaris rushed back to Louisville on Monday after the Derby for a scheduled meeting with the stewards the following morning when he would receive "official" notification of the Bute positive. Around 7:30pm on Monday, the trainer drove to Churchill Downs to check on Dancer's Image, and he saw some odd activity in Dr. Harthill's laboratory at the end of Barn 24. The veterinarian and Davis were standing at a table crushing some white pills into a coarse powder and then mixing the granules with oats in a partially full bag. Standing outside the feed stall, adjacent to the stall where

Dancer's Image was, Cavalaris was surprised a few minutes later to see Davis poke his head through a trap door in the back and toss in the oat sack.[94]

Cavalaris confronted Dr. Harthill, who told the trainer that "we were in trouble and had to do something." Cavalaris then examined the rest of his feed and came across a nearly full sack of bran that also contained white granules. He touched a bit of the white powder to his tongue and it tasted bitter, like aspirin or Bute. The trainer suspected that Dr. Harthill and Davis had tampered with the bran as well as the oats. Robert Barnard, who had gone to Barn 24 earlier in the evening and saw Dr. Harthill and Davis salt the bran, later confirmed Cavalaris's suspicions.[95] He had not tried to stop them because he assumed that Cavalaris was in on the plan, whatever it might have been.

The doctored feed was one of the main topics of conversation during a meeting the next morning at the Harthill Barn. The consensus was that the "salted" feed had nothing to do with the positive urine test of Dancer's Image, but that it still was evidence of something, although no one was quite sure just what. Ned Bonnie wanted to get the bran sack out of the barn to keep it "secure." Arthur Grafton told George Ralston, who worked for Dr. Harthill, "don't put it in Ned's car, put it in mine."

Accepting Grafton's position as senior counsel, Bonnie did not object. He later learned that Grafton had taken the feed and dumped it under a bridge somewhere in Oldham County, Kentucky. Grafton subsequently decided that had not been a wise idea, retrieved the bran sack and some of the feed and reported the incident.[96]

Davis's attorney, Millard Cox, called the salting scheme "phantasmagoria," and that was being overly kind to his client and to Dr. Harthill. Their convoluted thinking, according to Davis, was to allow Cavalaris and Barnard to see the crushed pills being added to the feed. If the trainer and his assistant had been the ones who slipped Bute to Dancer's Image before the Derby, they would try and clear themselves by reporting the doctored feed as an excuse for the positive drug test. At that point, Dr. Harthill and Davis would expose them as cheaters. If Cavalaris and Barnard were innocent, on the other hand, they would report the salting, and Dr. Harthill and Davis would reveal that the pills actually were aspirin and not Bute.[97]

Davis told the racing commission that his motive was to protect Dr. Harthill, apparently by deflecting suspicion away from the veterinarian and in the direction of Cavalaris and Barnard. The veterinarian said that he and Davis wanted to "test" Cavalaris, not to frame him.[98] Either way, the plan had little chance of success. Dr. Harthill and Davis apparently failed to take into account that, a few hours before they doctored the bags of oats and bran, investigators had conducted a thorough search of the premises. That search included the horse's feed and turned up no evidence of phenylbutazone. Finding grain laced with Bute or aspirin after that search would not prove anything useful about the positive drug test.

The incident had no relevance to whether Dancer's Image had been dosed with Bute prior to the Derby, but it did establish that nearly everyone involved distrusted nearly everyone else. Arthur Grafton even was initially suspicious of Ned Bonnie because of his long-standing friendship with Dr. Harthill and Davis

The salting fiasco also demonstrated how easily someone—Dr. Harthill or one of the other veterinarians who roamed the barns, Cavalaris or another trainer, a groom, a casual visitor or almost anyone else who knew their way around the backstretch—could get to Dancer's Image. Good or bad, track security was designed to keep intruders out, not to protect a horse from people already in the barn area with a legitimate reason to be there.

None of this proves anything, of course, and there is no evidence to suggest that Dr. Harthill's denial of involvement should not be taken at face value. Rumors and suspicions, by their very nature, are unfounded, and speculation without proof carries no weight at all.

Drug testing has improved dramatically since 1968, and today's technology probably could provide a definitive answer to the question of whether Sample 3956U actually contained traces of phenylbutazone. But there is no sample to test. There are no smoking guns.

Either Sample 3956U contained traces of phenylbutazone, or it did not. Kenneth Smith was adamant that it did, but Lewis Harris's independent tests called that assurance into question. Expert opinion was equivocal and not based on independent testing.

Perhaps the only incontrovertible fact is this: on the first Saturday in May 1968, in the seventh race at Churchill Downs, Dancer's Image ran faster than any other horse in the field and finished first in the ninety-fourth Kentucky Derby.

EPILOGUE

What is the real legacy of Peter Fuller and Dancer's Image?

It may be tempting to think of Fuller as a modern-day Don Quixote tilting at windmills, a sore loser finding imaginary villains in a hard-working racing chemist like Ken Smith, the stewards or the members of the racing commission. Conventional wisdom held that Fuller's was a fight that could not—and should not—be won. There was some sentiment that he should pack his bags and go back to Boston for the good of racing and for the good of everyone involved.

Quitting might even have seemed like a good idea at the time, with the hearings dragging on and the legal bills piling up. But Fuller was not a man to give up in the middle of a fight, especially a tough one. He was convinced that Dancer's Image deserved to be recognized as the legitimate winner of the 1968 Kentucky Derby, and he fought on.

In the process, he changed the face of racing forever.

Testing for prohibited drugs always was an odd mix of science and art, with strong emphasis on the latter. More often than not, racing chemists would emerge from their laboratories to announce a "positive," and the finding would be accepted without question simply because the chemist was the "expert," the only person qualified to interpret the test results. The results were accurate because the chemist said so. People might have wondered about the efficacy of drug testing before, but Fuller's challenge to Kenneth Smith was the first time that a racing chemist had been asked to prove to a scientific certainty that he actually knew what he was talking about. The result was an eye-opener: calling a test result "positive" and proving it

Despite the legal setbacks, Peter Fuller never lost faith in his horse. *Winants Brothers photo. Courtesy of the* Blood-Horse.

with objective scientific methods were two entirely different things. Racing chemists no longer can rely on their reputations and expertise. If a chemist says a test is positive, he must be able to prove it, often in a courtroom.

The extensive hearings and litigation surrounding the 1968 Kentucky Derby also established that parties embroiled in an administrative hearing are entitled to the same due process of law guaranteed a defendant in proceedings before a court. Most important was a decision by the Kentucky Court of Appeals that Fuller was entitled to prehearing discovery, the right to demand that the racing commission produce documents and other evidence relating to its conduct and that of the commission's official chemist.

Peter Fuller may have lost the battle, but he won the war. Testing procedures for the Kentucky Derby were revised, backstretch security at Churchill Downs was stepped up and the rules of racing were rewritten.

"Had Peter Fuller not stood his ground," said Edward S. Bonnie, one of the attorneys who challenged the racing commission, "we might still be in the Dark Ages when it comes to drug testing on the race track."

Peter Fuller's faith in Dancer's Image and his conviction that the horse was the legitimate winner of the 1968 Kentucky Derby have never wavered despite the years of frustrating and expensive legal setbacks. He always maintained that he sought vindication for Dancer's Image because he thought the horse deserved credit for finishing first in the most famous race in the world, and decades later, he still monitors press reports for anything he thinks is unfairly critical. When he comes across an item that is untrue or that casts Dancer's Image in a negative light, he contacts the editor and politely but firmly asks for a retraction.

In 1993, Fuller contacted Kentucky governor Brereton C. Jones, himself a successful owner and breeder of Thoroughbreds, and suggested that a public proclamation that Dancer's Image was the winner of the Kentucky Derby would be appropriate on the twenty-fifth anniversary of the race. "According to the law, he really is [the winner]," Fuller wrote. Governor Jones declined to make a public statement, but he replied in a letter to Fuller that "I absolutely recognize Dancer's Image as the winner of the 1968 Kentucky Derby."[99]

Fuller has never raced another horse in the Kentucky Derby, but he has been successful at other venues. A Fuller homebred, Mom's Command, won a number of Grade I races on the way to earning an Eclipse Award as the best three-year-old filly of 1985. Those victories were even sweeter because, in most of her races, Mom's Command was ridden by Fuller's daughter, Abigail. She had been the youngest of the Fuller children to accompany their father to Churchill Downs to watch Dancer's Image defeat Forward Pass.

A weathered billboard stands in one of the paddocks at Fuller's Runnymede Farm in New Hampshire. The billboard has huge photographs of Mom's Command and Dancer's Image, the latter identified as "WINNER" of the 1968 Kentucky Derby. Not surprisingly, if you know Peter Fuller, there is no asterisk by the horse's name.

***

Dancer's Image raced once more after the 1968 Kentucky Derby, in the Preakness Stakes at Pimlico Race Course in Baltimore, Maryland. He finished third, several lengths behind Calumet Farm's Forward Pass, but the Fuller colt was disqualified and placed eighth for bumping another horse,

Dancer's Image at stud in Maryland. *Winants Brothers photo. Courtesy of the* Blood-Horse.

Martins Jig. Ankle problems that had bothered Dancer's Image for much of his racing career forced the colt's retirement before the Belmont Stakes. In announcing the retirement, an emotional Peter Fuller told reporters, "Dancer's Image is too honest and game a horse to allow him to race in the Belmont and not be in perfect physical condition to give his best."

The horse entered stud with twelve official victories from twenty-four starts and with career earnings of $236,636. Although the original syndication plans for Dancer's Image fell apart after the disputed drug test was made public, Fuller subsequently engineered a deal for the horse to enter stud in Maryland in 1969. Dancer's Image later stood in Ireland, France and Japan. One of the leading sires in Japan, Dancer's Image showed signs of colic on December 25, 1992, and he died the next day at the age of twenty-seven.

***

Lou Cavalaris Jr. and Peter Fuller parted company a few months after the Kentucky Derby when the trainer disbanded his public stable to train for his main client, George Gardiner. Cavalaris was inducted into the Canadian Horse Racing Hall of Fame in 1995. A successful trainer for three decades and a prominent official at Canadian tracks, Cavalaris still attends the races on a regular basis. Dancer's Image was one of the best horses he ever trained.

***

Litigation aside, Robert N. "Bobby" Ussery remains one of only five jockeys to finish first in back-to-back runnings of the Kentucky Derby. The others are Calvin Borel, 2009 and 2010; Eddie Delahoussaye, 1982 and 1983; Jimmy Winkfield, 1901 and 1902; and Isaac Murphy, 1890 and 1891. Ussery was inducted into the National Museum of Racing's Hall of Fame in 1980.

Bobby Ussery and Dancer's Image after crossing the finish line first in the Kentucky Derby. *Winants Brothers photo. Courtesy of the* Blood-Horse.

From 1951 through his retirement in 1974, Ussery rode 3,611 winners from 20,593 mounts. When he retired, he ranked fifth among Thoroughbred racing's leading money winning riders. Ussery now works as a jockeys' agent. Dancer's Image was his last mount in the Kentucky Derby.

***

Forward Pass won the Preakness Stakes by six lengths and went into the Belmont Stakes three weeks later with the prospect of becoming the first Triple Crown winner to have been beaten in one of the three races in the series. Fears of Roger Maris–style asterisks in racing's record books were dispelled when Greentree Stable's Stage Door Johnny won the Belmont by 1½ lengths. At the end of the year, Forward Pass was voted champion three-year-old male in one poll; Stage Door Johnny got the nod from voters in the other two polls. Like Dancer's Image, Forward Pass eventually wound up as a breeding stallion in Japan, where he died in 1980. His success at stud did not match that of Dancer's Image.

***

Mrs. Gene Markey had been gracious after the positive test result for Dancer's Image first was announced: "I'm awfully sorry for Mr. Fuller. I don't know him personally, but some of my staff at the farm does and I'm sure he couldn't have had anything to do with a thing like that."[100] But as the hearings and litigation dragged on, she became less charitable and more critical. Calumet Farm never raced another winner of the Kentucky Derby, although Alydar came close in 1978 when he ran second to Affirmed in all three Triple Crown races. Mrs. Lucille Markey died in 1982, and her daughter, Bertha Wright, inherited the farm. She hired her son-in-law, J.T. Lundy, to run Calumet, and for a time, the operation continued to prosper. Questionable business decisions and the suspicious death of leading sire and moneymaker Alydar eventually forced Calumet into bankruptcy, and the farm was sold to the late Henryk de Kwiatkowski for $17 million at a public auction in 1992. Lundy wound up serving a prison term after convictions for fraud, bribery and conspiracy. A shadow of its former glory, Calumet now is operated by a trust for the benefit of de Kwiatkowski's children.

Epilogue

***

The gold trophy for the 1968 Kentucky Derby became merely another asset in the Calumet Farm bankruptcy proceedings. Dismayed at the prospect of the historic collection being sold off piecemeal, James E. Bassett III organized the Save the Calumet Trophies Committee. The committee raised a total of $2.7 million from private donations and the state. Several other potential buyers showed some interest in the trophies, but the committee wound up with the only serious offer. "It had to be done," Bassett said at the time. "It would have been a travesty, a tragedy and an embarrassment to the community, the state and the racing industry to permit the dissolution of this magnificent collection." Calumet's eight Kentucky Derby trophies are the centerpiece of a permanent exhibit honoring the historic farm in the Museum of the Horse at the Kentucky Horse Park near Lexington.

***

Dr. Alex Harthill was a popular and controversial equine veterinarian prior to the 1968 Kentucky Derby, and he remained so afterward. Dubbed the "Derby Doc," Harthill treated, by his own account, more than two dozen Kentucky Derby winners, from Citation in 1948 through Grindstone in 1996. Dancer's Image was the last Derby runner to be stabled in Barn 24, the controversial Harthill Barn. In 1972, amid growing criticism from just about everyone, the veterinarian moved his office from the Churchill Downs barn area. Harthill died in 2005 after suffering pneumonia and a stroke. He admitted treating Dancer's Image with phenylbutazone on the Sunday before the Kentucky Derby but steadfastly denied any involvement in the horse's subsequent positive drug test.

***

Phenylbutazone remains a controversial medication. The "zero tolerance policy" prevalent in 1968 has been replaced nearly everywhere by testing for acceptable threshold levels of the painkiller, but no one seems to agree on what those levels should be. The rationale for abandoning zero tolerance is that sophisticated chemical tests unavailable in the past now can detect miniscule residues of the drug in a horse's system long after any therapeutic effects can be felt. In fall 2010, the International Rules Committee of the Association of Racing Commissioners International approved reducing the threshold level from five micrograms/milliliter to two micrograms. The National Horsemen's Benevolent and Protective Association and several other groups opposed lowering the standard.

***

Drug testing rules for the Kentucky Derby were changed after the Dancer's Image debacle. In 1968, only the first place finisher and another horse selected at random were chosen, which eventually resulted in the winner's share of the purse and the trophy going to Forward Pass, a horse that had not been tested for illegal medications. In 1969, the first five finishers were tested, and the lab procedures were expedited to allow an announcement of the results on the day after the race rather than several days later. All of the tests were negative. In 1971, the Kentucky Rules of Racing were amended to clarify that a horse that tests positive for a prohibited medication would be considered unplaced for all purposes other than betting payouts. What the racing commission had done by fiat after the 1968 Kentucky Derby became a rule.

It now is standard procedure to split urine and blood taken from a horse into "A" and "B" samples. The A sample is used for immediate testing, and the B sample is retained if further testing is required. After the 1968 Derby, Peter Fuller requested a portion of the urine collected from Dancer's Image for testing by an independent laboratory. The request was refused because the sample collected from the horse had been used up in the initial tests or discarded.

***

The credibility and competence of Kenneth Smith came under repeated attack during many long hours of cross examination by Peter Fuller's attorneys after the chemist declared that Dancer's Image won the 1968

Kentucky Derby with phenylbutazone in his system. Smith continued working for the Kentucky State Racing Commission until 1975, when the contract with his company was canceled. He claimed that his rights were being violated when the testing contract was canceled, and in a strange bit of irony, he failed in an attempt to have the racing commission decision overturned in court. Years later, a bitter-sounding Smith told an interviewer: "Was I let go because of what happened after the '68 Derby? Absolutely."

***

Arthur Grafton, Stuart Lampe and Edward S. Bonnie returned to the respective legal practices. By the early 1980s, Ned Bonnie was being recognized as a "world authority on equine medication and the law."[101] Bonnie continues to practice law, and he continues to share his expertise on medication issues with racing and sport horse organizations. He was one of the people who helped write the first rule requiring split samples for drug tests.

***

Everyone knew that Dancer's Image crossed the finish line first in the 1968 Kentucky Derby, but lingering uncertainty over which horse would get official credit for the victory created a problem for the manufactures of the popular souvenir mint julep glasses sold at the track. Long a popular collector's item, the glasses traditionally included a list of all Derby winners. The glass issued for the 1969 Derby had no list of winners at all, and the 1970 glass had the name of Dancer's Image with an asterisk. Along the bottom rim of the glass was this explanation: "Dancer's Image's purse ordered redistributed to Forward Pass. An appeal to this order is pending." More recent Derby glasses list Forward Pass as the official winner, with no mention of Dancer's Image.

Appendix A

STEWARDS' PRELIMINARY
STATEMENT (MAY 7, 1968)

The chemist for the Kentucky State Racing Commission has reported that the analysis of the urine sample taken from Dancer's Image, winner of the seventh race May 4, 1968, contained phenylbutazone and/or a derivative thereof.

Pursuant to Rule 14.06, when said sample indicates the presence of such medication such horse shall not participate in the purse distribution, and under the Rules of Racing the wagering on said race is in no way affected.

By Order of the Stewards

Appendix B

STEWARDS' RULING
(MAY 15, 1968)

On May 6, 1968, the duly appointed chemist of the Kentucky State Racing Commission reported to the stewards that a urine test of Dancer's Image, the winner of the seventh race at Churchill Downs on May 4, 1968, contained a medication known as phenylbutazone and/or a derivative thereof.

In accordance with the Rules of Racing of the Kentucky State Racing Commission, Lou Cavalaris and Robert Barnard, the trainer and assistant trainer of the horse Dancer's Image, were duly notified, and at their request Monday, May 13, 1968, was assigned as a hearing date to consider and dispose of the matter.

A hearing was held on May 13, 14, and 15, at which times all affected parties were present in person or by counsel. After carefully considering all of the testimony and exhibits in the aforesaid hearing, the stewards are of the opinion and find:

1. Phenylbutazone and/or a derivative thereof was present in the urine of the horse Dancer's Image, winner of the seventh race at Churchill Downs on May 4, 1968, in violation of Rule 14.04 of the Kentucky rules of racing;

2. That the trainer and assistant trainer of the horse Dancer's Image, namely, Lou Cavalaris and Robert Barnard, respectively, were in attendance upon and had the care of the horse Dancer's Image and were responsible for the condition of the horse;

3. Pursuant to rule 14.06 of the rules of racing, the purse in the seventh race at Churchill Downs on May 4, 1968, shall be redistributed as follows:

First money, Forward Pass;

Second money, Francie's hat;

Third money, T.V. Commercial;

Fourth money, Kentucky Sherry;

The betting on the race and the payment of parimutuel tickets thereon shall in no way be affected.

4. By virtue of the investigation conducted pursuant to rule 14.05 and the hearing held, as foresaid, certain matters have been brought to the attention of the stewards which, in their judgment, warrant further investigation and action by the Kentucky State Racing Commission.

It is therefore ordered:

1. Lou Cavalaris and Robert Barnard, trainer and assistant trainer, respectively, of the horse Dancer's Image, and each of them is hereby suspended from participation in racing and denied the privileges of the grounds to and including June 13, 1968.

2. Pursuant to rules 14/06 and 23.01, the purse in the seventh race at Churchill Downs on May 4, 1968 shall be redistributed...

First money, Forward Pass;

Second money, Francie's hat;

Third money, T.V. Commercial;

Fourth money, Kentucky Sherry;

The betting on the race and the payment of parimutuel tickets thereon shall not be affected.

3. Other matters which have been revealed to the stewards by reason of the investigation conducted pursuant to rule 14.05 of the rules of racing and in the hearing aforesaid are deserving of further study, investigation and action, and are hereby referred to the Kentucky State Racing Commission for such purpose.

Appendix C

KENTUCKY STATE RACING COMMISSION (JANUARY 6, 1969)

COMMONWEALTH OF KENTUCKY

KENTUCKY STATE RACING COMMISSION

In Re: Appeal of Peter Fuller

Findings of Fact, Conclusions of Law, and Order

This is an appeal by Peter Fuller from the May 15, 1968 order of the Stewards of the Kentucky State Racing Commission at Churchill Downs, Kentucky, finding the presence of phenylbutazone and/or a derivative thereof in urine of Mr. Fuller's horse, Dancer's Image, following the Seventh Race at Churchill Downs on Saturday, May 4, 1968, The Kentucky Derby, and redistributing the purse to the exclusion of the owner of Dancer's Image. The Commission has carefully considered all the testimony, exhibits, and argument presented in fourteen days of hearings, commencing November 18, 1968 and concluding December 7, 1968. The Commission has considered the facts anew, completely independent of and without regard to the findings made by the Stewards. Upon consideration thereof, the Commission makes the following findings of fact and conclusions of law and enters its final order in accordance therewith.

Appendix C

Findings of Fact

On Saturday, May 4, 1968, the thoroughbred, Dancer's Image, owned by Peter Fuller crossed the finish line first in the Seventh Race at Churchill Downs, The Kentucky Derby, followed by Forward Pass, Francie's Hat, T.V. Commercial, and Kentucky Sherry, in that order.

A urine specimen was taken from Dancer's Image under the supervision of the State Veterinarian, L.M. Roach, DVM, in an eight-ounce bottle bearing Urine Sample Number 3956U.

Louisville Testing Laboratory, Inc., 1401 West Chestnut Street, Louisville, Kentucky, by contract does chemical testing on samples from thoroughbred races under the jurisdiction of the Kentucky State Racing Commission. Kenneth W. Smith is President of Louisville Testing Laboratory, Maurice K. Cusick is his laboratory supervisor, and James W. Chinn is one of his technicians.

During the performance of routine screening tests in the Mobile Laboratory maintained by Louisville Testing Laboratory at Churchill Downs immediately after the races on Saturday, May 4, 1968, James W. Chinn obtained a positive indication on a Vitali's Color Test.

Later that evening at the permanent laboratory at 1401 West Chestnut Street, Louisville, Kentucky, it was determined by Smith, Cusick and Chinn that the positive indication came from sample number 3956U.

During a period, commencing Saturday night, May 4, 1968 and ending Monday noon, May 6, 1968, five chemical tests were performed on Urine Sample Number 3956U by Kenneth W. Smith. These tests consisted of two color tests, Vitali's and Mandelin's, two crystal tests, with copper chloride and an ultraviolet spectrophotometric test in base and acid solutions. For confirmation each of these tests was performed again on the sample on Tuesday, May 7. Cusick and Chinn observed or participated in each of the five tests at least once. The sample was properly preserved until the conclusion of testing on May 7, 1968.

All of these tests gave the results of which phenylbutazone and/or a derivative thereof would give after having been administered to a horse and extracted from its urine. No other substance would give the same reaction as phenylbutazone and/or its derivative in all of these tests. The tests were sufficient to identify the presence of phenylbutazone and/or a derivative thereof in the urine of Dancer's Image.

The graph in the center of Stewards Hearing Exhibit No. 6, and the data produced on Commission Exhibits 5 and 6 were all produced from

Sample Number 3956U. The Vitali's test detected with the number 9 in Picture Number 1 from stewards Hearing Exhibit Number 6 was produced from Sample Number 3956U.

Kenneth W. Smith is an experienced chemist, particularly in the racing industry, having participated in analyses of samples from thoroughbred horses since 1942, and in analyses for phenylbutazone since 1962, and is competent to conduct the five tests performed on Sample Number 3956U.

Mr. Smith concluded from his testing that phenylbutazone and/or derivative thereof was present in Sample Number 3956U. On the basis of the results obtained by Mr. Smith, this finding was confirmed by Dr. Frank Ozog, Lewis Harris, and George Jaggard, three experienced chemists in the racing industry.

Phenylbutazone and/or derivative thereof was present in the urine of the horse, Dancer's Image, following the Seventh Race at Churchill Downs on Saturday May 4, 1968.

Dancer's Image had prominent ankles before he began his racing career, that is, ankles prone to predisposed to trouble under the strain and stress of racing. They were carefully watched and treated from the inception of his racing career by Louis C. Cavalaris, his trainer. The right ankle had begun swelling in early 1968 at Bowie Race Course in Maryland. It was x-rayed at the time of the Wood Memorial in New York by Dr. Girard and prior to and after the Kentucky Derby by Dr. Harthill. It was swollen on Saturday, April 27, 1968, and Sunday, April 28, 1968, and successfully treated by Dr. Harthill with the concurrence of Mr. Cavalaris upon the latter date with a four-gram dose of Butazolidin (the trade name for phenylbutazone). There was dramatic improvement on April 29, 1968, and the horse was in racing condition and worked out well. However, the condition of the right ankle had again deteriorated by Thursday morning, May 2, 1968, so much so that it was the worst it ever had been up to that time. The ankle was swollen and engorged, a condition known as red-hot osselet. Dr. Scanlan would have recommended to the Stewards that Dancer's Image be scratched. The ankle began dramatic improvement Thursday afternoon, was in good condition on Friday, May 3, 1968, and on Saturday morning and at the time of the race was in excellent condition and racing sound. The ankle remained sound after the race and through Sunday and Monday. However, by Tuesday, May 7, 1968, the ankle had reverted to its condition of the previous Thursday.

Phenylbutazone is a potent anti-inflammatory drug for the treatment of certain painful inflammatory conditions and its use is generally manifest by prompt relief of pain and diminution of swelling, tenderness and local heat.

Phenylbutazone is the medication of choice in veterinary medicine for the condition of the right ankle of Dancer's Image on Saturday and Sunday, April 27 and 28, 1968, and Thursday, May 2, 1968. There is no other medicine known to have the dramatic effects of this drug in the treatment of such a condition. The known dose of phenylbutazone on Sunday, April 28, 1968, was dramatically effective in relieving and improving the condition of the right ankle the following Monday and Tuesday. The dramatic change in the condition of the right ankle from Thursday, May 2, 1968, through Saturday, May 4, 1968, was consistent with and what is to be expected from the use of phenylbutazone in veterinary medicine. The use of phenylbutazone contributed to the sound condition of Dancer's Image when he raced on Saturday, May 4, 1968.

Effective use of phenylbutazone will dramatically improve the condition and health of a horse with a phenylbutazone treatable condition. It affects the speed of a horse to the extent that it enables him to race when he would not otherwise be able to do so. It enables him to perform to his full potential when otherwise he would not be able to do so. Prohibition of the use of phenylbutazone is necessary in order to preserve honesty and integrity in racing because the indiscriminate use and withdrawal of the medication with many horses would vary their performance in racing. The rules of racing are designed to prevent use of medications and other devices for such a purpose.

Regardless of the amount of phenylbutazone and/or derivative thereof in the urine of Dancer's Image on Saturday, May 4, 1968, its presence in any amount shows that the administration affected the health and speed of the horse by enabling him to run racing sound.

Conclusions of Law

The Commission concludes as a matter of law that phenylbutazone and/or a derivative thereof was present in the urine of the horse, Dancer's Image, following the Seventh Race at Churchill Downs on May 4, 1968, in violation of Rule 14.04 of the Kentucky Rules of Racing; that pursuant to Rule 14.06 of the Rules of Racing. The purse in the Seventh Race at Churchill Downs on May 4, 1968, should be redistributed as follows:

1st money	FORWARD PASS
2nd money	FRANCIE'S HAT
3rd money	T.V. COMMERCIAL
4th money	KENTUCKY SHERRY

Under the Kentucky State Rules of Racing which governed the Derby race on May 4, 1968, the foregoing ruling does not affect the order of finish. The betting on the race and the payment of parimutuel tickets thereon should in no way be affected.

These Rules are within the authority granted the Commission under Chapter 230 of the Kentucky Revised Statues.

Order

IT IS THEREFORE ORDERED, pursuant to Rules 14.06 and 25, that the purse in the Seventh Race at Churchill Downs on May 4, 1968, shall be redistributed as follows:

1ˢᵗ money	FORWARD PASS
2ⁿᵈ money	FRANCIE'S HAT
3ʳᵈ money	T.V. COMMERCIAL
4ᵗʰ money	KENTUCKY SHERRY

The betting on the race and the payment of parimutuel tickets thereon shall in no way be affected.

Entered this 6ᵗʰ day of January, 1969, at Lexington, Kentucky.

KENTUCKY STATE RACING COMMISSION

George E. Egger, Chairman
Laban P. Jackson, Vice Chairman
John A. Bell, III, Member
Jean S. Friedberg, Member
Stanley W. Lambert, Member

Notes

Introduction

1. Herb Goldstein, "Bob Ussery 'Didn't Need Hunches,' Or Whip Either," *Daily Racing Form*, May 6, 1968.
2. Kenneth E. Loomis, "Dancers' [*sic*] Image Case Is Not At Finish Line," *Louisville Courier-Journal*, April 26, 1970.

1. The Commoner and the King

3. Information about the cost of living in 1964 was gathered from several Internet sources, including www.americanheritage.com and www.thepeoplehistory.com.
4. Eisenberg, *Native Dancer*, 256.
5. Biographical information was gathered from several sources, including Melvin Maddocks, "The Inner Life of a Wealthy Warrior," *Sports Illustrated* (May 23, 1977) and summaries from the National Governor's Association and the Fuller Foundation.

2. Thoroughbreds and Blondes

6. Barney Nagler, "Uncertain Racing Prospect Renamed," *Daily Racing Form*, May 4, 1968.

7. Lou Cavalaris's early recollections of Dancer's Image are taken from his sworn statements and testimony.

8. Nagler, "Uncertain Racing Prospect Renamed."

9. Chew, *The Kentucky Derby*, 100.

10. Commission hearing transcript, Keeneland Library, Lexington, Kentucky, vol. 1, 78.

3. No Good Deed Goes Unpunished

11. Jim Bolus, recorded interview, Kentucky Derby Museum, Louisville, Kentucky.

12. Ibid.

13. K'Meyer, *Civil Rights*, 136.

14. Garrow, *Bearing the Cross*, 560.

15. K'Meyer, *Civil Rights*, 136.

16. Governor Edward Breathitt's recollections of events surrounding the 1968 Kentucky Derby can be found in an interview conducted as part of the Kentucky Historical Society Oral History Project, available at http://205.204.134.47/civil_rights_mvt/pop.aspx?type=1&asset=384.

17. Garrow, *Bearing the Cross*, 571–72.

4. The Derby Doc

18. Bolus, recorded interview.

19. Ibid.

20. Jim Bolus, "The Alex Harthill Story," *Louisville Courier-Journal*, September 1, 1972.

21. Information about Dr. Harthill's checkered history was gleaned from a variety of sources, including reports in the *Blood-Horse*, the *Louisville Courier-Journal* and the *Daily Racing Form*. Among the more comprehensive sources of information are "The Alex Harthill Story" and Doug McCoy's "Dr. Harthill, Mr. Hyde," which appeared in *Thoroughbred Racing Action* in August 1990, 24.

22. Tom Easterling, "Dancer's Image Loses Derby Purse," *Daily Racing Form*, May 8, 1968.

5. The Most Exciting Two Minutes in Sports

23. Deposition of Robert Barnard, files of attorney Edward S. Bonnie, 11.

24. Whitney Tower, "And the Last Was First," *Sports Illustrated* (May 13, 1968).

25. Tom Easterling, "Forrest Predicts Sub 2:00 Derby," *Daily Racing Form*, May 2, 1968.

26. "Valenzuela Recast In Substitute Role," *Daily Racing Form*, May 4, 1968.

27. Joe Hirsch, "Forward Pass' Derby Stock Soars With Fine 1:376 Mile," *Daily Racing Form*, May 1, 1968.

28. Commission hearing transcript, vol. 10, 229.

29. Ibid., 212.

30. Ibid., 221.

31. Deposition of Lou Cavalaris deposition, files of attorney Edward S. Bonnie, 43.

32. Commission hearing transcript, vol. 4, 161–64.

33. Joe Hirsch, "Lavin's Imposts If Derby Were 'Cap," *Daily Racing Form*, May 4, 1968.

34. Commission hearing transcript, vol. 1, 82.

35. Joe Hirsch, "Derby Day Sidelights," *Daily Racing Form*, May 6, 1968.

36. Dr. Harthill's recollections of Derby Week are taken from a variety of sources, including his testimony at hearings conducted by the stewards and the Kentucky State Racing Commission. Medications administered to Dancer's Image by Dr. Harthill are reflected in an invoice sent to Peter Fuller covering the period from April 26, 1968, through May 6, 1968, reproduced in the *Chicago Tribune* on August 18, 1968.

37. Goldstein, "Bob Ussery."

38. Ibid.

39. Tom Easterling, "Great! Couldn't Dream It! Wonderful! Says Fuller," *Daily Racing Form*, May 6, 1968.

40. Ibid.

6. Welcome to Oz

41. Gail Evans, "Hands Knew Their Colt Had It Made," Louisville *Courier-Journal*, May 5, 1968.

42. Jim Bolus/Associated Press, "Method Of Testing Explained," *Lexington Leader*, May 8, 1968.

43. Whitney Tower, "It Was a Bitter Pill," *Sports Illustrated* (May 20, 1968).

44. Ibid.
45. This account of events at the mobile laboratory and at Louisville Testing Laboratory's Chestnut Street facility is gleaned from often contradictory testimony given at hearings conducted by the stewards and the Kentucky State Racing Commission.
46. Tobin, *Performance Drugs*, 389–90.
47. The conversation was variously reported as involving a sample that was "suspicious," a "suspicious positive" and a definitive "positive." The characterization of the sample as "suspicious" was made during sworn testimony before the racing commission.
48. Tower, *Sports Illustrated* (May 20, 1968).
49. Commission hearing transcript, vol. 5, 20.
50. Ibid., 13.
51. Ibid., 35, 69.
52. Ibid., 39–40.
53. Commission hearing transcript, vol. 3, 208, and vol. 5, 17, 73.
54. Tower, *Sports Illustrated* (May 20, 1968).
55. Bolus, recorded interview.
56. The full text of the stewards' preliminary statement may be found in Appendix A.
57. Tom Easterling, "Pain-Killer Found in Urine Analysis," *Daily Racing Form*, May 8, 1968.
58. Commission hearing transcript, vol. 5, 14.
59. Ibid., 92.
60. Joe Hirsch, "Dancer's Image Case Remains Unresolved; Hearing Continues," *Daily Racing Form*, May 14, 1968.
61. The full text of the stewards' ruling may be found at Appendix B.

7. AN UNBELIEVABLE WITNESS

62. Edward S. Bonnie, personal communication with the author.
63. Hirsch, "Dancer's Image."
64. Commission hearing transcript, vol. 1, 77, 83, 92–95.
65. Kent Hollingsworth, "The Story Does Not End There," *Blood-Horse*, November 30, 1968.
66. Commission hearing transcript, vol. 3, 205–06.
67. "The Great Derby Incident," *Chemical Engineering News* (May 20, 1968), 104.

68. Commission hearing transcript, vol. 4, 92.

69. Ibid., vol. 4, 127, 84–85.

70. Ibid., vol. 12, 79–82, and vol. 13, 129, 99–100.

71. Stewards' hearing transcript, Brief for Appellee, *Kentucky State Racing Commission v. Fuller*, Court of Appeals of Kentucky, File No. W-168-71, Kentucky State Archive, Frankfort, Kentucky, vol. 1, 73, 354, 367.

72. Commission hearing transcript, vol. 3, 16.

73. Ibid., 84.

74. The full text of the commission decision may be found in the Appendix C.

75. Commission hearing transcript, vol. 4, 63, 156.

76. Brief for Appellee, 221–26.

77. Memo Opinion, *Fuller v. Kentucky State Racing Commission*, Civil Action No. 75154, (Franklin Circuit Court, December 11, 1970), 3.

78. Ibid., 5–6.

79. Ibid., 6.

80. *Kentucky State Racing Commission v. Peter Fuller*, 481 S.W.2d 298 (Ky. 1972).

8. The Holy Grail

81. Actions by the new racing commission were taken from court records on file at the Kentucky State Archives in Frankfort, Kentucky.

82. Maryjean Wall, "Forward Pass 'Not Disturbed' as Calumet Gets Derby Gold," *Lexington Herald*, July 20, 1973.

9. The Usual Suspects

83. Commission hearing transcript, Opening Statement of Arthur Grafton, 7.

84. Commission decision, January, 7, 1969 press release, Kentucky Department of Public Information, Frankfort, Kentucky, 4–5.

85. Commission hearing transcript, vol. 10, 47–49.

86. Joe Hirsch, "Fuller Strongly Backs Cavalaris," *Morning Telegraph*, May 9, 1968.

87. Tower, "It Was A Bitter Pill," *Sports Illustrated* (May 20, 1968).

88. Associated Press, "Drug Scandal Robbed Dancer's Image of 1968 Kentucky Derby Title," May 3, 2008, Fox News.com, www.foxnews.com/printer-friendly-story/0,3566,354056,00.html.

89. This incident was widely reported and was confirmed during personal communications with Billy Reed.
90. Ibid.
91. Loomis, "Dancers' [*sic*] Image."
92. Bolus, recorded interview.
93. Bolus, "The Alex Harthill Story."
94. Details of the "salting" incident are derived from sworn testimony by the people involved and from affidavits prepared by attorneys Arthur Graton and Edward S. Bonnie.
95. Whitney Tower, "Inquiry…," *Sports Illustrated* (July 1, 1968), summarizing confidential (at the time) stewards' hearing transcripts.
96. Bonnie, personal communication with the author.
97. William F. Reed Jr., "Whitewash in Kentucky," *Sports Illustrated* (February 17, 1969).
98. Ibid.

EPILOGUE

99. Materials in the Jim Bolus archives at the Kentucky Derby Museum.
100. Easterling, "Pain-Killer."
101. Tobin, *Performance Drugs*, xiii.

SOURCES

Trying to piece together the facts surrounding events that happened more than forty years ago can be a dicey proposition at best. Documents vanish, memories fade, people pass away. Aside from a few weeks before and after the 1968 Kentucky Derby and on a few significant anniversaries of the race, relatively little has been written about Dancer's Image. Today, the horse is most often mentioned as a footnote to racing history, a fading memory of what might have been.

Source material for this book included a body of excellent contemporaneous reporting by *Blood-Horse* editor Kent Hollingsworth, columnist Joe Hirsch and his colleagues at *Daily Racing Form*, Whitney Tower at *Sports Illustrated* and journalists Billy Reed and Jim Bolus, along with the official transcript of the racing commission hearing, archived material at the Kentucky Derby Museum in Louisville and the Keeneland Library in Lexington and official court documents stored at the Kentucky State Archives in Frankfort. Whenever possible, the sources for direct quotations are noted.

Peter Fuller graciously gave the author permission to review material in the files of attorney Edward S. Bonnie.

Readers interested in additional background might consider the following books:

Bolus, Jim. *Kentucky Derby Stories.* Gretna, LA: Pelican Publishing Co. Inc., 1993.

————. *Run for the Roses, 100 Years at the Kentucky Derby.* New York: Hawthorne Books, 1974.

Chew, Peter. *The Kentucky Derby, The First 100 years.* Boston, MA: Houghton-Mifflin, 1974.

Eisenberg, John. *Native Dancer, The Grey Ghost: Hero of a Golden Age.* New York: Warner Books, 2003.

Garrow, David J. *Bearing the Cross, Martin Luther King Jr., and the Southern Christian Leadership Conference.* New York: W. Morrow, 1986.

K'Meyer, Tracy E. *Civil Rights in the Gateway to the South.* Lexington: University of Kentucky Press, 2009.

Landers, T.A. *Professional Care of the Racehorse.* Lexington, KY: Blood-Horse Publications, 2006.

McEvoy, John. *Great Horse Racing Mysteries, True Tales from the Track.* Lexington, KY: Blood-Horse Publications, 2000.

Staff of *Blood-Horse* Publications. *Horse Racing's Top 100 Moments.* Lexington, KY: Blood-Horse Publications, 2006.

Tobin, Dr. Thomas. *Drugs and the Performance Horse.* Springfield, IL: Charles C. Thomas, 1981.

A videotape of the 1968 Kentucky Derby and the complete *Daily Racing Form* chart for the race can be viewed at http://www.kentuckyderby.com/history/year/1968#full-recap.

ABOUT THE AUTHOR

Milt Toby is an author and attorney who has been writing about Thoroughbred racing for almost forty years. His five previous books include a biography of the ill-fated filly, Ruffian, and his short fiction has garnered national recognition. Milt is a director of American Horse Publications and chair of the Kentucky Bar Association's Equine Law Section. He lives in central Kentucky with his wife, Roberta, and a menagerie of assorted dogs and cats. Visit his website at www.miltonctoby.com.

Visit us at
www.historypress.net